Praise for "Hear Us Roar!"

"If you're a woman at a crossroads, then read Hear Us Roar!—it will leave you feeling encouraged, inspired, motivated, and proud"

—Kellie Greene, Speaker, Activist, and Founder of SOAR® (Speaking Out About Rape)

"The idea and ideals in this book are truly profound, on so many levels. I love the concept of amplifying women's voices, individually and collectively ... of featuring stories that so beautifully exemplify the journey from trauma to triumph ... and of offering the opportunity for authors and readers to come together in philanthropic support of those who deserve to access their "roar" and for us to hear it. Everyone benefits from this magnificent vision. My gratitude and kudos to author Andrea Howe, and all of the courageous women who shared their stories with authentic heart and generosity of spirit. Bravo!"

—Marcy Cole, Ph.D, Holistic Psychotherapist, Executive Director of First Tuesday USA, and Founder of First Tuesday Circle of Giving

(Turn the page for more reviews)

"I was touched, inspired and transformed as my journey through each woman's story unfolded. Though each journey differed, the essence throughout was the same—each author is an amazing, inspirational warrior and their stories will inspire, uplift and empower other women on the path to persevere"

—Linda Joy, Publisher, Aspire Magazine.

"Hear Us Roar! goes beyond the typical inspiration; it is truly a book packed with strength, courage and compassion. It shows us that when we, as women, think we cannot possibly go on ... when we think we have nothing left to offer ... we do go on. We rise, we heal, we create. Reading Hear Us Roar! is a gift you can give yourself—one that will keep giving throughout your lifetime"

—MaryEllen Tribby, CEO/Founder of www.WorkingMomsOnly.com and Publisher/ CEO of Early To Rise

HEAR US ROAR!

28 STORIES OF EVERYDAY WOMEN LEADING EXTRAORDINARY LIVES

XOXO
Andrea Howe
2010

Conceived and Edited by
ANDREA HOWE

Andrea Howe
1725 Eye Street Northwest, Suite 300
Washington, DC 20006 USA

1-800-946-4395 | info@hear-us-roar.com | www.hear-us-roar.com

Limits of Liability and Disclaimer of Warranty

This book is dedicated to my mom, Nicole.

Thank you for loving me, always,

and for teaching me that not all roars sound alike.

Table Of Contents

A Charitable Cause . . . . **i**

Acknowledgements . . . . **iii**

Meet Andrea . . . . **vi**

Chapter 1: Why Whisper When You Can Roar? **1**

The Invitation To Roar 2

A Roar Heard 'Round The World 3

Real Women, Real Stories 4

Why They Chose To Roar 5

Chapter 2: What Makes These Women Powerful? **9**

Four Keys To Standing In Your Power 9

Gratitude: An Unexpected Theme 10

Chapter 3: Perseverance 11

Eight women share about the power they found in **meeting life and its challenges one day, one step at a time,** and in doing so show us what's possible when determination and resolve triumph over circumstance.

Maureen O'Brien 15

Kimberly Whitehead 18

Allene Brack 22

Christine Tully 25

Chrissy Turner 28

Ina 32

Gillette 35

Lee Ann Price 37

Chapter 4: Authenticity 41

The seven women chosen for this chapter are role models for **being true to yourself, especially when it requires a willingness to defy conventional wisdom**. Learn about the unexpected results of daring to follow your heart.

Robin Barbier 44

Mandy Gordon 47

Lauren Malmon 51

Natalie Jobity 53

Yael 56

Cindy Colucci 58

Ginnie 60

Chapter 5: Faith 63

For some of the seven Roar authors featured in this chapter, faith is tied to believing in themselves—their own innate wisdom or "center." For others, it is about God. For others still, faith stems from more amorphous divine presence. In all cases, these women placed **deep trust in themselves or something larger**, and created powerful partnerships with inspiring results.

Kelly O'Brien 66

Sheila 69

Ellen 71

Janis Goad 75

Emily Hinson 78

Maimah Karmo 81

Rita Lombardo 83

Chapter 6: Generosity 87

The Roar definition of generosity is **making a difference for others; giving back**. The six stories selected for this chapter are particularly illustrative of the power of seeing beyond the confines of your own experience to reach for the infinite rewards that come from acting with compassion, courage, and bigheartedness.

Katherine Stone 90

Erica Rueschhoff 92

Jaime 95

Cathy Barber 98

Shannon 99

Anne Pellicciotto 103

Chapter 7: Awakening the Roar 107

How Roaring Changed One Woman's Life 108

The Time Has Come to Hear You Roar 108

Post Script: Andrea's Story (and a Glimpse at the Roars Yet to be Heard) 111

Book Club Questions for Discussion 115

Bibliography 116

Author Index 117

A Charitable Cause

The Hear Us Roar! project was born out of a commitment to making a difference by creating a powerful community of women who raise money for their charities of choice through the sharing of their stories.

By buying this book, you have joined a remarkable community of women committed to making a difference by contributing directly to the charities selected by our Roar authors. For the 28 women featured in this book, these charities include:

American Red Cross

An Infinite Mind

Associação Frei Gregório, Cabadelo, Brazil

Breakthrough Corporation

Child Welfare League of America

Children's Hospital & Research Center Foundation

Coalition for Improving Maternity Services

Conscious Living Radio/Drishti Point Program

DC Impact

Dress for Success

Foodshare, Bloomfield, CT

Friendship Missionary Baptist Church/International Children's Outreach Ministry

Homes that Change Lives

Inspiration Alumni Foundation

Journey of Hope/The Campaign for Healing, Caring and Comforting

Oprah's Angel Network

Overeaters Anonymous

Postpartum Support International

Race to Walk

SADS (Sudden Arrhythmia Death Syndrome)

Sharing Sorrows ... Healing Hearts

SOAR® (Speaking Out About Rape)

THEARC (The Town Hall Education Arts & Recreation Campus)

Tigerlily Foundation

Women's Resource Center/Putnam County, NY

Acknowledgments

Hear Us Roar! is a project created by a small and mighty group of entrepreneurial women living throughout the U.S. We borrow our inspiration from Margaret Mead, the famous anthropologist who said, "Never doubt that a small group of thoughtful, committed citizens can change the world. Indeed, it's the only thing that ever has."

Members of the Roar Team include:

Andrea Howe, President and Founder of BossaNova Consulting Group

Gillette Conner, International Development Professional

Kelly O'Brien, Creator of TurningPointe and Designing a Life

Mandy Gordon, Communications Consultant

Vickie Turley, Owner of A Balanced Alternative

Our heartfelt thanks go to others who have offered their talents and contributions, most with little or no compensation:

All the Roar authors, for their enthusiasm, passion, generosity and commitment to making a difference;

Aletha McManama of DC Virtual Office Solutions, for designing and maintaining the first Hear Us Roar! web site;

Anne Pellicciotto of SeeChange Consulting, for her editing and outreach advice;

Ashley Dobbs of Keep the Promise, whose partnership kept me marching forward;

Danielle Taylor of Taylor Made, for her PR and social networking expertise;

Donna Kozik of MyBigBusinessCard.com, for the structure and coaching that made this book a reality;

Elizabeth Kenney of Virtual E Business Solutions for her early role on the Roar Team, and her authentic support of the project;

Erica Rueschhoff of MomsRealLifeUniversity.com for her enthusiastic offers to help ... any time, all the time;

Jacki Opferman of JMO Administrative Services, for website updates and virtual assistance;

Kay Gilley, for her gentle wisdom and insight into the power of the number 28;

Knight Kiplinger, for his publishing and blurb know-how;

Kym Johnson of KSJ Marketing Communications, for the initial Roar logo concept;

Landmark Education, for the personal breakthroughs that led to the genesis of this book;

Lisa Winston, for her encouragement and proofreading prowess;

Mark and Beth House, for offering their mountain retreat so this book could be born in beautiful surroundings;

Martin Brossman, for being such a strong advocate for women everywhere;

Nicolette Pizzitola of Compass Point Associates, for her unwavering commitment to women and to the completion of this project;

Rachel Roizen, for her bright, shining spirit and her social media and marketing expertise;

Ruby Holden, for "listening" this book into existence;

Ryan Lanigan of RL Design, for the original Roar logo and tag line, book cover and layout;

Virginia Sambuco, for being an extraordinary catalyst.

Meet Andrea

Women are making remarkable strides in the world. We are fully expressing our natural ability to lead with beauty, grace and a collaborative spirit. It's also true that we still diminish, downplay and underrepresent our own abilities and accomplishments.

I am no exception. I am 41 years old at the time of this writing and just beginning to truly embrace my power—as a leader, businesswoman, entrepreneur, colleague, daughter, sister, friend and life partner. In many ways, the Hear Us Roar! project is a reflection of my own journey to share my voice and speak my truth.

The genesis of the Hear Us Roar! project was my "coming out" at the age of 38 as a rape survivor, when I created a program called *Living Out Loud* that offers improv comedy workshops to survivors of sexual violence who are ready to laugh again (www.lolworkshops.com). Within six months of its inception, *Living Out Loud* was given a prominent mention in SELF magazine and acquired by a national nonprofit.

My experience with *Living Out Loud* totally boosted my confidence as a leader and left me with no doubt that sharing — roaring! — is transformational. I've lost count of how many survivors have come out to me after hearing my story — including my mom, who silenced her own experience of rape for 60 years. Through *Living Out Loud*, my single voice liberated my own spirit and touched those nearest and dearest to me, along with thousands of others.

"Hear Us Roar! 28 Stories of Everyday Women Leading Extraordinary Lives" is intended to be the first in a series of publications that provides a way for "ordinary" women to step into their power and to *stand* in it. It is my most sincere wish that, through this book and the others to come, women around the world will discover this: that authentically sharing our struggles and our victories brings freedom, joy and inspiration to storytellers and listeners alike.

The time has come to Hear Us Roar!

Chapter 1: Why Whisper When You Can Roar?

Have you ever met a woman who is obviously exceptional and everyone knows that about her but her? Your sister is "supermom;" your co-worker is a corporate star; your girlfriend is an adventuress and lover of life. Yet when you acknowledge her for her accomplishments, she brushes it off or changes the subject. I'm not talking false humility here; I'm talking an actual inability to really see how great she is. Like the anorexic who looks into the mirror and sees *fat*, these women make an extraordinary difference in their families, their workplaces, and their communities—sometimes simply by *being who they are* — and see "average," or nothing, when they look at their own reflection.

It's a pervasive problem. And it isn't just their problem. If you're a woman, then chances are you struggle with at least some variation of it. Case in point: When was the last time you really let a compliment sink in?

It's true that women are making remarkable strides in the world to fully step into our natural leadership roles — as moms, volunteers, politicians, CEOs and everything else in between. We are increasingly appreciated for our natural abilities to listen, bond, inquire, attend to detail, speak and act from our beliefs, and use our intuition.

It's also true that we still diminish, downplay, and underrepresent our own abilities and accomplishments. We compare our challenges and struggles to others' and, in so doing, discount our victories as well as our trials. We carry secrets that weigh us down. We don't share our stories because we don't think they matter. And the world suffers as a result. Women are, after all, the cause of life itself. Whether a woman ever becomes a mother, she still brings her maternal gifts to bear on the world and on future generations. Her drive to create is a force of nature.

It's one thing for female celebrities and Fortune 500 executives to use their star power and clout to change the world. This project is not about them. Hear Us Roar! provides an opportunity for "ordinary" women, as individuals and as a collective, to step into their power and then *stand* in it. By sharing their triumphs, our Roar authors declare themselves to be the powerful women they are. By buying this book, together we celebrate the strength and power of women across the globe while simultaneously raising money for charity.

Read on to meet 28 remarkable women who share the secrets to turning your whisper into a roar. Be moved by what you read. And discover yourself in the process.

The Invitation to Roar

In the summer of 2008, the Roar Team used the power of the Internet (www.hear-us-roar.com) to offer an invitation to women around the world:

> *Tell us about a time in your life that you shook hands with your own power. It might have been a single defining moment—an event or experience. Or perhaps it was more subtle; a process over time. But in the end, the result was the same: you stepped back and saw clearly the powerful person you are. Then you stepped forward and embraced your power.*

We asked each author to give us a sense of who they are, including what led up to their awakening, what's different now as a result — for themselves and for others — and why they chose to share their story. We dared them to move us and others with their sharing. And they did.

Oh, and we asked them to do it in 1200 words or less.

In return, we promised to raise $100,000 for the charities of their choice through the sale of books and other Roar-related products.

A Roar Heard 'Round the World

Within four months of issuing the Invitation to Roar we collected 84 stories from three continents. This was an extraordinary response, considering that Hear Us Roar! is an all-volunteer, grass roots effort. Without the benefit of corporate sponsorship or a PR firm working diligently in the background, the Roar Team had only our networks and our belief in the passion and generosity of women around the world to rely on. Both proved reliable.

One woman in Kenya named Gemma was so committed to submitting her story that she retyped 1,000+ words into her Blackberry when she had difficulty accessing the Internet. Here's what Gemma told us:

> *"Dear Andrea: Sorry I couldn't attach my story. I am out in the field in Kenya so our Internet is dodgy and I won't have access 'til next week. It's also nearly 2am! Heather just sent me this and I know it's due. So you'll have to accept it from my Blackberry in the body of my next email. I've never sent anything this large so I hope you get it with no formatting issues. This Blackberry typing is definitely challenging!"*

What a beautiful example of a commitment to making a difference.

Gemma is not alone. Here is a list of the 63 locations from which our 84 story contributors have roared:

Africa ... Alexandria, Virginia ... Altamonte Springs, Florida ... Annapolis, Maryland ... Austin, Texas ... Baltimore, Maryland ... Bethesda, Maryland ... Bethlehem, Pennsylvania ... Bloomfield,

Connecticut ... Bloomfield Hills, Michigan ... Brownfield, Texas ... Burke, Virginia ... Burnaby, British Columbia ... Canton, Massachusetts ... Charlotte, North Carolina ... Columbia, Maryland ... Dallas, Texas ... Duncanville, Texas ... Durham, North Carolina ... East Hartford, Connecticut ... Eugene, Oregon ... Falls Church, Virginia ... Fayetteville, Georgia ... Framingham, Massachusetts ... Gold Hill, North Carolina ... Goodyear, Arizona ... Jupiter, Florida ... Lakewood, Colorado ... Leesburg, Indiana ... London, United Kingdom ... Madison, Alabama ... Mesa, Arizona ... Mission Viejo, California ... Mount Airy, Maryland ... Mount Kisco, New York ... Nairobi, Kenya ... Newburgh, New York ... Ninety Six, South Carolina ... Oak Park, Illinois ... Oakton, Virginia ... Old Bridge, New Jersey ... Pacific Grove, California ... Paducah, Kentucky ... Port Jervis, New York ... Reston, Virginia ... Rockville, Maryland ... Roswell, Georgia ... Saint Louis, Missouri ... Salisbury, North Carolina ... Santa Monica, California ... Scarborough, Maine ... Suttons Bay, Michigan ... Takoma Park, Maryland ... Tampa, Florida ... Toronto, Ontario ... Vienna, Virginia ... Walnut Creek, California ... Washington, DC ... Wayne, New Jersey ... Wethersfield, Connecticut ... Williamsburg, Virginia ... Winchester, Virginia ... Winter Park, Florida

Real Women, Real Stories

Our Roar authors aren't celebrities and they aren't professional writers; they are real women sharing themselves in a very real way. Indeed, the purpose of the Hear Us Roar! project is to provide an opportunity for "ordinary" women to share themselves so that other "ordinary" women would catch a glimpse of their own reflection. Here's what we wrote in our invitation:

> *Consider this: there are probably at least a dozen other women on the planet who are facing circumstances like yours but don't have the gift of your perspective. They can't yet see the opportunity in front of them. Or they can but their fear is holding them back. What if you knew there was the smallest possibility that your story could be the catalyst; the mirror that allows another woman to see herself in a new light, understand that she's not alone, and take action to claim her power? What if, by sharing your story, you enable just one woman to experience herself and her life in a whole new way? While you may ask yourself, "Who am I to share?" the real question is this: who are you not to share?*

Our story selection process was simple. We used four basic criteria:

1. **Is it readable/logical; does it flow?**
2. **Is there a clear connection to power?**
3. **Is there a "You Go Girl" factor?**
4. **Could another woman with a similar challenge read this story and see a clear pathway for herself?**

In the end, the 28 stories included in this book are those that clearly met the criteria above, required little or no editing to go to press, and also fit together well as an introductory collection.

We've also included anecdotes and quotes from all 84 contributors to give you a sense of this amazing community.

Why They Chose to Roar

Here's what a few of the 84 Roar authors had to say about why they chose to submit their stories:

> *"My commitment to the empowerment of women led me to share my story"* — Gloria

> *"We all have a story. I have always been moved to share my story, my highs and my lows, in the hopes that I would help transform someone else's life. I believe that there are experiences we undergo, endure or triumph through that seem to be miraculous, lucky, random, or even undeserved so that we serve as a channel through which the knowledge, wisdom and skills acquired can be transferred to another who is walking or will walk the path that we have just tread. By sharing, we are blessed"* — Kimberly

> *"I feel privileged to have the opportunity to be part of such an inspiring and consciousness-shifting project and movement. So often in the world we only hear about the tragedies and the 'victims,' and so little voice is given to the triumphants and heroines. Now through this project we open the door for the heroines of this world to be heard ... and to roar"* — Karen

"I was inspired to share my story by the stirring example offered in the invitation—and by my knowledge that extraordinary goals can be accomplished when we reach out to each other, bare our souls, and strive for something that is nearly impossible to reach by ourselves" — Deborah

"In sharing, there is unity and in unity, we are not alone" — Liz

"There is a vitality, a life force, a quickening that is translated through you into action, and there is only one of you in all time, this expression is unique, and if you block it, it will never exist through any other medium; and be lost. The world will not have it. It is not your business to determine how good it is, not how it compares with other expression. It is your business to keep it yours clearly and directly, to keep the channel open. You do not even have to believe in yourself or your work. You have to keep open and aware directly to the urges that motivate you. Keep the channel open"

—Martha Graham, Choreographer

Chapter 2: What Makes These Women Powerful

At first, every Roar story seemed impossible to categorize—how do you confine a story of hope, triumph, courage and strength into one "bucket?" After several attempts over several months, four clear themes finally emerged.

Four Keys to Standing in Your Power

Here are the four themes that consistently made it possible for our first 28 Roar authors to awaken their inner roar:

- **Perseverance.** Meeting life and its challenges one day, one step at a time;
- **Authenticity.** Being true to yourself, especially when it requires a willingness to defy conventional wisdom;
- **Faith.** Placing deep trust in yourself or something larger than you;
- **Generosity.** Making a difference for others; giving back.

The stories you will read in the pages to come have been grouped accordingly. As you read them, you'll certainly see evidence of more than one theme rippling through each one — for example, the word "faith" appears many times in our Authenticity stories. Each story was categorized based on the theme that seemed to amplify her roar the most.

Gratitude: An Unexpected Theme

As the Roar Team culled through the stories that were submitted from around the world, we were surprised by an unexpected thread that was woven through so many: the expression of gratitude. Many Roar authors actually shared appreciation and gave thanks for the tragedies and traumas they faced. In fact, it seems the greater the difficulty, the deeper the gratitude. Here are some examples:

> *"I not only forgive my ex-business partner for ruining my business and suing me, I thank her profusely for it. Because my experience with her and my failed business made me look at my life and see it in a way I had never seen it before"* — Lee Ann
>
> *"I'm so grateful that such a devastating experience led to work that is so meaningful to me"* — Katherine
>
> *"I am very thankful for the experience of breast cancer in my life. I am thankful that it has propelled the real me to show up in my life, as a woman, as a mother, and a citizen of the world"* — Maimah

What an extraordinary demonstration of the kind of women you are about to get to know through the stories to follow — women with gigantic hearts and expansive spirits.

Be prepared to be touched moved, and inspired by the women on the pages to come.

Chapter 3: Perseverance

***"When your dreams turn to dust, vacuum"*—Author Unknown**

In 2005, a year-long study conducted by Caliper, a Princeton, New Jersey-based management consulting firm, and Aurora, a London-based organization that advances women, identified key characteristics that distinguish women leaders from men. One of the four specific conclusions about women's leadership qualities was this: "When feeling the sting of rejection, women leaders learn from adversity and carry on with an 'I'll show you' attitude." Similar findings are echoed in Esther Wach's book "Why the Best Man for the Job is a Woman: The Unique Female Qualities of Leadership." Here the author profiles the working styles of 14 executive women, including eBay's Meg Whitman, Ogilvy & Mather's Shelly Lazarus, Ingram Industries' Martha Ingram and Bain & Company's chairman, Orit Gadiesh, to learn what makes them so successful. One quality that bubbles to the top is the determination to turn challenges into opportunities.

We call this perseverance — **meeting life and its challenges one day, one step at a time** — and that's precisely what the Roar authors selected for this chapter so beautifully illustrate. Their challenges are unique and consistently daunting: from tirelessly overcoming financial challenges to fighting a years-long battle with depression to making the slow and steady climb to earn a late-in-life college degree.

Prepare to meet eight extraordinary role models who will show you what's possible when determination and resolve triumph over circumstance.

Meet Maureen. Maureen was inspired to roar as a way of exposing the truth behind the "success stories" of working women. She writes, "I've scanned profile after profile of women who have exceeded their profit margin or helped the world on a major scope or published a best-selling children's book. Some of these stories offer an inkling of the path it took to get there, but it's usually given the short shrift." Read about Maureen's path to her own definition of success that included stops in corporate America, entrepreneurship, a brush with The Oprah Show, and cancer.

Meet Kimberly. A first-generation American born to a family from the West Indies, Kimberly came into the world with high expectations for a life full of opportunity. Her steady stream of accomplishments were thwarted when her secret burden — a family that couldn't afford her success — grew too heavy. Kimberly says, "I found myself in a lost place." Find out how several years (and several degrees) later, Kimberly's mentoring of students facing similar struggles led her to discover her "core genius."

Meet Allene. Allene was a widow, an empty-nester, and at a crossroads. Determined to answer the nagging internal question, "Who in the world am I?" Allene did what was unthinkable for a 46-year-old woman with a shaky sense of self-worth in 1984: she enrolled in college. She started with Geometry I and, step by step, made her way to nursing school — only to fail her final exam many classes later by .04 points. Find out how Allene's story ends and why she says, "Any goal can be reached if you refuse to give up."

Meet Christine. Christine was a shy, soft-spoken petite woman who didn't fit anyone's idea of a military officer. Yet she found herself the only female in a class of 50 during Navy Officer Candidate School, a grueling 13-week break-you-down and build-you-back-up experience.

"The only problem was that I broke down a little too much," says Christine. "I started crying and barely stopped ... it was beyond embarrassing." Her lack of confidence attracted drill instructors in droves. Find out how Christine's determination — and heart — resulted in a journey come full circle.

Meet Chrissy. Chrissy was on a business trip to South Florida when a date rape drug was put in her drink. Waking up on the side of the road, robbed and left for dead, she thought it was the end of life as she knew it. Chrissy says, "Everything I was taught growing up, to respect and trust others, to believe there is more good in the world than evil, no longer existed." Read about the six-year recovery that led to the discovery of her purpose in life.

Meet Ina. In her early 20's, Ina was determined to create a happy life with her intended husband. But making ends meet was a struggle, working $6 per hour jobs with three-hour commutes (one way). Then hopes for liberation through a home-based business opportunity were dashed when a scam was uncovered and $2,000 in loan money was lost. Ina says, "By the time it was all said and done, we were in debt with the bank, behind on rent, and on our last leg." Find out what happened in the two years that followed and why Ina says, "To those who have been through Hades on earth, remember that there is a Lioness in all of us. Sometimes it just needs to be awakened!"

Meet Gillette. Gillette echoes the importance of "steady as she goes" in her story of a two-year battle with depression. She says, "I found myself at the bottom of a pit, realizing only too late that I had fallen into a rabbit hole too smooth to climb out of without some help." But knowing you need help and having the energy to get it are two different things, so there she was, living 3000 miles from home, crying or sleeping for close to 18 hours a day and getting by on the other six. Learn about the empowering realization that led to Gillette's first step up and out of that hole, and her gradual ascent until she could see light.

Meet Lee Ann. Just five months after opening a meal assembly kitchen, Lee Ann had 150 loyal monthly customers and was poised to make a profit long before she was projected to. Then one night the phone shook her out of sleep at 2:30 a.m.—a fire in a nearby store resulted in the indefinite closing of Lee Ann's business, and an order by the Board of Health to destroy all the food. This turned out to be just the first of a string of challenges and letdowns that ended with a closed business, failed business partnership, four lawsuits, and personal bankruptcy. Find out why Lee Ann asserts, "Wherever you are on your life journey it can be better. In fact, if your mindset is right, it *will* be better. The best is always yet to come."

Hear Maureen Roar

Why I've chosen to share my story. Sometimes I feel like my roar is stuck in my throat. Or that what I'm trying to achieve is a roar-in-the-making, but it's not quite audible yet. (If you roar in the forest and no one is there, can you still hear it?)

The interesting thing is that other people probably consider me quite successful; in fact, I've often chatted with other working moms who say they envy the career path I've chosen. Why the disconnect?

Like most women, I'm much harder on myself than anyone else is. My sense of achievement has been high for as long as I remember, and I'm definitely a self-starter. Yet, at some level, my self-confidence is always challenged by circumstances beyond my control.

That's what's driving me to write my story. Whenever I read "success stories" of working women, it's always after-the-fact. I've scanned profile after profile of women who have exceeded their profit margin or helped the world on a major scope or published a best-selling children's book. some of these stories offer an inkling of the path it took to get there, but it's usually given short shrift. To me, the journey is the key to unlocking their success and I'm just as intrigued by their failures. So I'm going to share mine, in the hopes of motivating all the other women out there quietly pursuing their goals.

What life was like before. From the American Dream perspective, my life on paper in 2005 was a success story. My roots stemmed from the blue-collar ideals and Irish Catholic mentality of a close-knit family, one that was full of Boston Irish cops. Yet from the beginning I challenged the stereotypes of my youth. I became the first in my clan to graduate from college, then married a Cuban (gasp, NOT Irish) man with whom I have two wonderful sons. Along the way, I received my PhD, wrote a book and held several good-paying jobs with mother's hours. What more could I ask for?

Apparently, corporate stability. My company was bought out by venture capitalists whose values, shall I say, did not mirror mine. It took hiring a lawyer and months of grief to get the severance package that was due to me. (Lesson #1: Never meet with a "transitional VP" behind closed doors; it'll be your word versus his.) This detour led to my first defining moment: I am not in control of the business environment (or the ethics of those around me), but I can be in charge of my own career choices.

With this cash flow as my seed money, I started my own consulting business, Destination Parenting. The timing felt right: "Nanny 911" was all over the TV, helicopter parenting was the buzzword, and overscheduled kids were everywhere. I had faith that my unique brand of humor, advice and experience would help legions of other parents.

My leap of faith, it turns out, had another unexpected stumbling block: cancer. Which brings me to Lesson #2: You can't control the timing of bad news. On November 1, 2006, the very day that I was supposed to be launching my business, I was instead under anesthesia, having part of my cancerous colon removed. Talk about a side step. The way I look at it, there are two ways to treat the irony of that moment: either I wasn't really meant to pursue this new career track (or the cancer diagnosis was a colossal STOP sign being waved in my entrepreneurial face), or God was putting things into perspective for me. Being a stubborn, Irish-Catholic I chose to go with the latter interpretation.

Oddly, the day I came home from the surgery, the phone rang, and my son said "It's 'The Oprah Winfrey Show,' Mom." Thinking it was a joke, I answered and it truly was Oprah's producers, calling for one of my clients, who would be featured on an upcoming show! "That's more like it," I said to myself, "if Oprah isn't a sign that this new career track is going to pay off, what is?"

Lesson #3: Sometimes the Big Break ... isn't. So, did the Oprah event turn into my big break, complete with overwhelming awareness of my business? Unfortunately, no. I wasn't asked to be on the show; the producers just wanted behind the scenes expertise. It was a wake-up call, though, in that it demonstrated the importance of keeping your name "out there" even as you pursue your own path. In the process of starting my own company, I've maintained relationships with colleagues, I've done lots of pro bono media work, and I've even spent time behind the lowly 8' x 10' table at my neighborhood mall. Some of the opportunities have turned into actual money-making activities, but many have not. (In fact, so far, most have not.)

In reality, I need look no further than the bathroom mirror if I'm searching for a scapegoat for why I'm not the female Dr. Phil (yet!). Have I taken advantage of EVERY opportunity out there? Have I pounded the pavement incessantly and blogged my way into the public's eye? Do I have hundreds of clients knocking down my door? No.

On the other hand, have I received requests for workshops from people who've heard me speak recently or have read my parenting articles? Yes, several. Have I made a significant difference in the lives of the parents who have come to me for individual coaching for their wayward children? Yes", they say, "we're better off now." That's a milestone in-and-of-itself.

The bottom line, then, depends on how we each define success. If it's the biggest splash, or the loudest roar, I'm surely not there yet. If it's waking up each day putting forth some effort on my (still) fledgling business while I juggle all the other tasks of ordinary life — elder care, carpooling and, occasionally, the gym, I'd say I'm holding my own nicely.

In fact, on the day of my two-year cancer-free anniversary, I may let out a small, private roar of my own. I hope you find your own milestone and join in.

Maureen O'Brien, PhD is a developmental psychologist, parenting coach and mother of twins. Dr. O'Brien is a sought-after consultant to individuals, companies and the media on child development and parenting issues. She is the founder of Destination Parenting (www.destinationparenting.com) and the author of "Watch Me Grow: I'm One-Two-Three." Her writing and workshops are dedicated to confident, successful childrearing.

Hear Kimberly Roar

We all have a story. I have always been moved to share my story, my highs and my lows, in the hopes that I would help transform someone else's life.

I believe that there are experiences we undergo, endure or triumph through that seem to be miraculous, lucky, random or even undeserved so that we serve as a channel through which the knowledge, wisdom, and skills acquired can be transferred to another who is walking or will walk the path that we have just tread. When we share, we find that the empowerment bestowed upon us is ricocheted back to our essence, as it feeds life, healing, freedom and peace to our cores. Just by sharing, we are blessed.

I have realized that it is not only my life's mission, but my purpose to share, empower, mentor, inspire and transform.

This is my story.

The creation of my life's canvas began in 1978 when I emerged, lungs wailing, in a diminutive five-pound, nine-ounce package. Even then, it seemed as though I had something to share. As a first-generation American of a family from St. Vincent and the Grenadines in the West Indies, the hope for a fabulous, enriched, opportunity-seized life was born.

A child with a shy demeanor, I found it strange when family members, teachers, mentors and sports coaches would marvel at the seeming ease and proficiency at which I excelled academically, athletically and musically. After all, what else does a child do other than express herself naturally? Truly, stemming from a family of educators, nothing less was desired or expected. A smile, a "thank you", and often, an inward embarrassment at the attention would ensue, and I (and my talents) would continue contentedly along towards another class, another practice, another accomplishment. This was my story. And then it ended.

I flew through elementary and secondary school, graduating from a prestigious independent boarding school at 16 years of age. I enrolled in the Biomedical Engineering degree program at the University of Pennsylvania, steamrolling on the path towards success. Or so I thought. What could be wrong? There I was, at an Ivy League university, enrolled in a groundbreaking academic program, and living amongst my peers. The truth is that I had a burden—a secret burden—passed down from my family, without intent, but nevertheless, with impact. I couldn't afford school.

Working was not new, as I relished the day when I turned 14 so I could obtain my "working papers" and buy what I wanted. As it often occurs with first-generation students and their families, I enrolled, un-mentored and unguided, in the financial aid and scholarships system. Family funds were often sent to relatives who were planning their own ways to be able to come to the United States and jumpstart their dreams. Parental contributions were figuratively existent but unrealistically unavailable.

While grants certainly covered the bulk of tuition costs, there were several thousand dollars left unmatched per year. It is a normal rite of passage to meet living expenses in the form of a work-study job. I began my collegiate journey with not one but several work-study jobs under my belt balancing the load of a challenging curriculum. Quickly, I found myself in a lost place. I tutored students, but was many times too tired to perform well on long, intensive exams myself. Academic achievement was slipping through my fingers. When I learned about scholarships and opportunities for internship, leadership and development programs, I could not qualify with my grade point average. Semesters became more frustrating as I internalized the experience and its impact on my self-esteem. However, the essence of who I was remained unchanged. A scholar is always, to the core, a scholar. An achiever, in her heart, will always be an achiever.

I persevered. My outlet and supplementary education came in the form of music. In the fall of my sophomore year I joined The Inspiration, a university-sponsored performing arts group with the purpose of promulgating the history and culture of the African Diaspora through a cappella music. I graduated from Penn with a degree in Biomedical Engineering, and a double minor in

Psychology and African-American studies, weathering close calls, but determined to succeed. I persevered to attain my dreams and enrolled in Georgetown University Law Center to obtain my law degree. Friends and family often joked that I was a lawyer before I became an attorney. The frustrating circumstances continued as my collegiate grade point average did not qualify for many scholarships that would have allowed me to focus fully on my academic studies in law school. A repeating cycle ensued with a dream almost deferred. God's blessings and victory found their way into my experience as I graduated with my J.D. and became a patent attorney at a Top 100 firm. I discovered the merger of my love for science and law.

Despite the transcripts' apparent depiction of my talents, my professors, deans, dorm masters and employers buffered me as I weathered a challenging situation. I was not and would not be the first student to enter the hallowed halls of these institutions with a similar situation. As they succeeded, so would I. I did. I have.

In keeping with my life's purpose, I have shared my story and advice to friends and family members who were walking or aiming to walk a similar path. Engineering and law students alike (and their parents) receive financial planning, academic and mentoring advice from me. This is my passion. This is my core genius. This is part of my purpose – to clear the path for those behind me.

My yearning to make a difference bled over from one-on-one relationships to one of a broader impact. In furtherance of the legacy of scholarship, service and edutainment, I founded The Inspiration Alumni Foundation, Inc. (IAF), a nonprofit scholarship organization borne out of my experiences as a student-musician, and a joint desire among our alumni to promote the synergy between the arts and higher education. Our charge is to provide financial assistance to non-arts majors in college and graduate school who supplement their traditional academic curriculum with dedicated membership in university-sponsored performing arts groups.

Through programs such as cable channel VH1's "Save The Music", there is a resurgence of support for music programs in elementary, middle and high schools across the nation. Yet, as soon as these budding young men and women enter college and university academia to pursue degrees in science, education, law, business and the humanities, the emphasis on the importance of the study, the performance of music as a companion to a traditional non-arts curriculum, is all too quickly forgotten. The IAF recognizes that these students' academic achievements, leadership skills and well-being are enhanced by their participation in extracurricular arts programs on their campuses.

As Chair of the organization, the chapters of my story continue to unfold. I am excited about the impact on the lives of aspiring scholar-musicians and the ricocheted healing, deliverance, peace, and purpose it will bring to our souls.

This is just the beginning of the journey that God has in store for me. I am poised for projection into my destiny.

Kimberly Whitehead is an attorney specializing in intellectual property. As an entrepreneur herself, her passion is in educating business owners on investing in their ideas and protecting them through patents, trademarks, and copyright. She is the founder of The Inspiration Alumni Foundation Inc. (www.theinspirationfoundation.com) Kim can be reached at kbwhitehead@cox.net.

Hear Allene Roar

My story, if experienced today, would probably not hold as much merit as it did in 1984.

That year I was 46 years old, a widow for seven of those years, and at a crossroads in my life. Between the empty-nest syndrome and the persistent questions like, "Who in the world am I?" and "What am I doing here?" I felt that I had some decisions to make.

Learning has always interested me and "college" seemed to come out of somewhere that I can only describe as God-sent. But I was 46, and college girls were 18, fresh out of high school, and full of 12 years of preparation and knowledge.

Scared to death and feeling very elementary, I got through enrollment and shyly entered the office of the counselor, who handed me a sheet of algebra problems and asked, "Do you remember any of this?" To my surprise, I did! He said "Okay, you will be in Geometry 1" and before I left his office, I had 18 hours of study scheduled, not really having any idea what I has gotten myself into. But he said that he believed I could do it, and I guess he convinced me that I could! How did he know?

I soon became the grandmother of all 18-year-olds and the first (it seemed) non-traditional student. The first two semesters I completed the required study of curriculum, still not sure in which direction I was to go. The most dreadful thing in any college year was money and that was an issue with which I had to deal. Pride was set aside as I became a member of the "displaced homemakers," a source of grant monies and wonderful, never-ending encouragement. Even there I was the "senior" displaced person, but respect took on new meaning for the other participants, the counselors, the instructors and for me.

In this setting, I began to find myself and realize my own self-worth. This was very new and exciting! I felt there was nothing I could not do.

Imagine my anxiety when the call came for me to become a nurse! I definitely was not that smart! In church, I had always heard that God never calls you to a task that he does not also provide the preparation. I did not see how I could be that prepared! But then, through much soul-searching, instructor persuasion and peer encouragement, I applied for nursing school and took the entrance exam.

Hallelujah!!!! I received the highest score of those who applied and I was off to start a career — a real career! Never would I say that nursing school was easy; it not only challenged me, it awakened something in me that I never knew was there. What truly miraculous things are the human body and mind! How I looked forward to each day's word, chapter, and subject!

"You never have a mountaintop experience without a season of let-down" — this saying never meant more than when, in my last semester, I failed my final exam by .04 points. I was devastated! I was a total failure! Once more, I was challenged to try again. I could sit out for a semester and re-enter for the last semester and do it over, or I could continue in school and complete an Associate Degree in science. I was persuaded to complete the few hours I needed for the science degree and was then ready to enter nursing again that spring. This time, success was mine and in the process I had earned two degrees with only one minor set-back (looking back, of course).

Next came the most frightful experience of all — the Board of Nursing. In Louisville, where the Kentucky exams were held, there were students from all over the state with a million different emotions flowing in, around and through us — mostly fear. The conductors of the event were as frightening as the exam itself, so much so that even breathing was an almost-stifled necessity.

The dread lasted much longer than the eight hours of testing because we then had to wait six weeks for results. My hands shook so hard when that day came and I opened the mailbox. There it was — that important, brown, official-looking envelope. Panic turned to joy as I read "passed" on the letter. I read it many times that day.

Thus the "Who in the world am I?" question was answered and my life as a registered nurse began at one of our two local hospitals. Finding out 'why' I was here was indescribably realized. I found meaning, purpose and complete fulfillment as I ministered to the sick and dying. Gratitude for life, both the patient's and mine, grew with each pill, each injection, each tear, each prayer and each sorrow as new friends passed in and out of my life's work.

After 13 years, I retired at age 64 and then served part-time for two years at a nursing home. Even yet, deep inside of me beats the heart of a nurse and it will continue because that is who I am.

My story is incomplete, but I have saved the best for last. When my husband died, I was only 39. One by one, my four children left the home, some even moving out of state. I was left with such nothingness, like the hollow empty shell one looks for on the beach with no life inside. But my girls have always been in my court; they are the force behind my drive to be all that I can be. With their encouragement and support, how could I ever be anything other than an achiever? The most joyous memory that I have is walking upon the platform to receive my nursing diploma and there in the front row sitting together were my four young, beautiful, wonderful daughters. Above the roar of the crowd, I could hear clearly "Atta girl, Mama! Way to go!" I still hear it today.

Finding oneself after seemingly having no identity can be and often is a difficult time, but once the questions are answered, there is no stopping — maybe side-stepping, but no stopping.

Any goal can be reached if you refuse to give up.

Allene Brack is now a 71-year old nursing retiree from Western Kentucky, with much to roar about. Four daughters and as many sons-in-law, 15 grandchildren and eight great-grandchildren make her "den" quite the joyful crowd at family gatherings. Overall, her roar is of a life who has trusted in a God who is bigger than any wound, any setback or upset, and is the center of all that she is or can be. Allene's motto is, "Whatever the age or station in life, each new sunrise is cause for roaring."

Hear Christine Roar

"I viewed it as a challenge," I heard myself say, in a voice more rich and expressive than I normally spoke in.

My statement was technically true but conveniently omitted how I felt about challenges. As I looked around the room, I was surprised to see that my classmates actually appeared to be interested in my speech.

Three weeks had passed since reporting to Navy Officer Candidate School, a 13-week commissioning program for college-educated enlisted sailors and civilians, and I was finally starting to adjust.

At Officer Candidate School, the members of the graduating class become "Candidate Officers" one week prior to receiving their commission. One of their duties is to indoctrinate the incoming class. Upon my arrival, I was immediately surrounded by Candidate Officers barking orders at me and forcefully instructed to restring my shoelaces in very specific ways while yelling answers back and maintaining a 1000-yard stare.

I think the objective was to give you a lot of simple but rapidly given instructions that you could do under normal circumstances but become unable to do due to stress, and then make you feel bad about it. "How can you become a Naval Officer when you can't even get this right!" It wasn't difficult to convince me; I already had serious doubts about my ability to lead others.

The break-you-down-and-build-you-back-up approach is common and effective in military training environments. The only problem was that I broke down a little too much. I started crying and barely stopped during my first week. It was beyond embarrassing. I wanted so much to stop but just couldn't. The irrational yelling triggered some kind of response in me, and my usual coping mechanisms of hiding and blending in didn't work; they got me through enlisted boot camp, but only leaders were welcome here and leaders don't hide.

I began to see something new in the faces of the Candidate Officers: worry. They didn't want me to fail; I was the only female in a class of 50. As a shy, soft-spoken, petite woman I knew I didn't fit anyone's idea of what a military officer was.

The lack of female classmates didn't help. There were two female Candidate Officers that embodied the strength, assurance and military bearing that I aspired to. They made sure I connected with other women in the program and secretly fed me cookies in the bathroom, although at the time it didn't appear to help much — whenever someone was nice to me it just made me cry harder. They arranged for me to meet a woman who had been on hold for over a year due to an injury, and was considered the resident expert on the program. She told me funny stories and helpful advice such as: if you want the drill instructors to leave you alone, just carry a tampon around. I laughed through my tears and reflected on the determination it must have taken to stay in the program that long, voluntarily. I didn't believe I could make the 13 weeks, let alone a year.

It didn't get any better when the Marine drill instructors took over. These were men that are every bit as intimidating in person as they appear to be in movies. They are also as funny as they are portrayed in the media although they'd better not catch you laughing at their jokes until around week six. Not surprisingly, I drew a lot of attention, and there's no such thing as good attention from a drill instructor in the first few weeks of training. I had a classmate that went through most of the program without the drill instructors knowing his name. That was not going to be an option for me, even without all the tears. My lack of confidence was attracting drill instructors to me in droves. I didn't know that confidence was what I was missing, but then I wouldn't miss something I never knew what it felt like to have.

The speech was kind of a turning point for me. It was an exercise during a lesson on public speaking. We submitted three possible topics and they would pick which one we discuss. I thought they would pick our topics randomly but later I realized I would naturally be assigned "What it's like being the only female in class." It was the first time in my life that an oral presentation had gone well. I spoke about the positive aspects (I had my own room) as well as the negative (felt isolated) and the neutral (men and women are different, which earned me hearty guffaws, like "Oh really? You think?").

Later, there were other turning point moments, like when our class drill instructor Gunnery Sergeant Jones pulled me out in front of a classmate that resembled a bodybuilder and asked him why I was still doing push-ups and he wasn't. He answered his own question: "Heart. She has heart." Of course the push-ups I was doing by then could hardly be called push-ups, they were so bad. But I was still trying and he was right, I had heart. I was determined to make it through.

The class dwindled from 50 to 17, due to failed inspections, physical fitness tests or academic exams. Some sustained injuries and a few chose to leave the program. With the help and support of a lot of people, I did make it through. And I never fell out during a formation run, even the crazy Saturday morning ones to cadences about napalm.

I felt like I came full circle when I was designated as the Candidate Commander in charge of indoctrinating the new class. I wished I could tell my cookie-sharing role models how much their concern meant to me, but they had long since transferred to their new duty station.

After the commissioning ceremony, our class Chief Petty Officer told us that there will be times in our naval career when we look back and wish that things were as easy as they were in Officer Candidate School. He was right. It was the just beginning of a long process for me. Even as I write this, part of me worries that it doesn't fit what a Naval Officer is supposed to be. But most of the time I don't worry about what I'm supposed to be anymore. It's like waking up from a long sleep and thinking how much the world around you has changed, except it hasn't changed — you have.

I started taking acting classes, something that I never would have been able to do before. I found that it's possible to be yourself whatever environment you happen to be in. And I found a place where my tendency to cry might actually come in handy: on stage!

Christine Tully separated from the Navy in 2008 and is currently supporting the Navy as a contractor and taking Improvisation classes at the Studio Theatre Acting Conservatory in Washington DC. Christine can be reached at cktully@optonline.net.

Hear Chrissy Roar

I'm Chrissy, a 44-year-old mother and wife, but most importantly a confident, strong and happy woman again (finally). This is my story.

In November of 2002, I was on a business trip in South Florida when a date rape drug was put in my drink. I just wanted to unwind with a drink and watch the sunset at a local beach bar, but a stranger had other plans. Fortunately, I don't remember the actual rape. After my exam found seven lesions in my uterus, I was sure I didn't want to.

Waking up on the side of the road, robbed, left for dead, trying to figure out what happened to me was bad enough. I never thought it could happen to me! It was definitely the end of life as I knew it. Everything I was taught growing up — to respect and trust others, to believe there is more good in the world than evil — no longer existed and felt completely unachievable.

No one I confided in reacted the way I thought; no one knew how to help. I felt desperately abandoned by the world. I went into hiding while I questioned everything about myself, my family, my friends and especially my faith. It was undoubtedly the biggest demon I ever had to deal with and I can honestly say now is one of my biggest accomplishments to have overcome.

Six years later, I am happily married to the most wonderful man in the world and life has never been better. If you would have told me back then that life would be this good now, I would've laughed in your face (if I could even remember how to laugh and actually get the strength up).

Don't get me wrong, my life was never the same after the rape. But I did still have a life — albeit completely different — and had a defining moment (and a lot of small ones afterwards) that made me decide to make the most of what I had left. In the process, I found my purpose in life and became a rape counselor. Going on four years now I've volunteered at my local crisis center and counsel sexual abuse victims and their families when they come in to get their rape kit. When

I'm not on call, I'm helping survivors on a daily basis all over the world through my website, www.dealingwithrape.com. The number one question I get is, "How did you deal with it?" While everyone is different and I try to help with suggestions, I always tell my story in the hopes that it brings some encouragement and optimism.

I'll never forget the day it happened — not the rape, but the day I claimed my new life. It was positively one of the best days of my life. It was the day I transformed from victim to survivor. After almost having a nervous breakdown, I had finally gotten the courage to seek counseling. After several months of self pity (which I totally deserved and couldn't believe I was paying for when I was obviously a pro at home for free), my counselor told me about a book (a true story) that she wanted me to read.

It took me a while to buy the book — the last thing I wanted to read was about someone else going through what I did (let alone spend money on it)—but I finally did. I went home to my free, fully-equipped self-pity pad and decided to do my homework.

Well, I never got past the first paragraph, not because I don't like homework (which I don't) but because I didn't need to; I had read enough. The first paragraph is about a woman who had just been brutally raped and was giving her statement to the police. The officer told her she was lucky because the girl found in the same spot prior had been killed and dismembered. (Not to be gory but it really happened.)

That is when I had my epiphany; when I least expected it, everything fell into perspective. All of a sudden there was this weight lifted from my shoulders. I noticed it was a beautiful day and the sun was shining. I started looking at things differently. I started to cry and for the first time in a long time they were happy tears. I realized that, even though I had felt dead all this time, I wasn't, and I had a choice to make: I could either continue to act dead or I could live the life I had left.

I chose life and never wanted it more. I thought to myself, "I don't think God left me on this earth to let my attackers dictate and control how I live my life," which is what I'd been doing. The rape controlled my thoughts, my security, how I dressed, how I acted, where I went or more often where I wouldn't go (thank God for online shopping). Not anymore! Enough had been taken from me and I wasn't giving up another second of it because I realized *it's my life* to control—no one and nothing else but me! I guess I should have also added "stubborn" in my introduction because I was fired up and all I wanted to do was prove to myself and everyone else that I was in control. I couldn't believe how powerful I felt. I wanted to scream from the rooftop to the world that I'm alive!

The day I realized I literally could be dead gave me a whole different viewpoint. I saw that I was throwing away my future by being consumed with things I couldn't change from my past. I decided to stop with the coulda-shoulda-woulda and transfer all that energy and work to what I *could* control.

That day I wrote down short- and long-term goals defining what I did and did not want in my future, and then took baby steps to get there. It didn't happen overnight and it wasn't all smooth sailing, but the fact that I was in charge of my body and life was the most powerful step towards my recovery. I knew what I went through was horrific but I refused to let it define me anymore. And once I began to keep my mind on my goals (no matter how small they were), things started to fall into place.

A year later I met my husband. I told my story to him the first night we met and instead of running scared like the others (bastards — that's for all of us, had to say it) he embraced me and saw my strength instead of my weaknesses. We've had four years of happiness, trust, support, deep love and wonderful sex (yes I said it!) I'm not bragging (well, maybe), just trying to give hope to anyone who thinks it is unobtainable. Anything is obtainable if you really want it, work at it and don't give up on yourself.

I thank God every day for giving me the strength to help myself and offer guidance to other victims so they become survivors and live happily again.

In 2007, Chrissy Turner joined the speaker's bureau of Speaking Out About Rape, Inc.® (SOAR®). SOAR runs national awareness, education and prevention programs to empower survivors of sexual violence and enhance the public's understanding and acceptance of rape victims. As a member of TEAM SOAR® Chrissy shares her personal story of rape, healing and hope. Chrissy was named The United Way's Tampa Bay Volunteer of the Year for Human Services in 2008 and in 2009 was recognized and honored as one of five of Tampa Bay's Local Heroes by Verizon Yellow Pages of Tampa for her work at The Crisis Center of Tampa Bay.

Hear Ina Roar

I was told about Hear Us Roar! by a friend, Martin Brossman. I want to share my story because, for my age, I have seen and done a lot of things, and I've been at low points that I pray no one else ever has to experience.

My "awakening" came in the fall nearly two years ago. I was living in North Carolina at the time, with the man I will be marrying. We are young — I am only 24 and he is 22. At the time, we had just rented an apartment in Chapel Hill, the home of the University of North Carolina and a pretty expensive little town. The apartment was small, almost like a cave, but it was the first thing we'd been able to pay for on our own. We both worked a hideous shift at Raleigh's airport, arriving at 4 a.m. and working until 1 p.m., earning only about $6 per hour each. It was rough, but we did get tips here and there and it was just enough to maintain our little place.

This is when the downward spiral started. We got the notice that the contract company we were working for would be shutting down soon because it had lost its contract. It wasn't so bad for me to leave because of how severely I hated the job. We were responsible for helping disabled passengers get through security and to or from their planes. Any little thing done wrong could have meant a hefty monetary fine and legal action, yet we were expected to be courteous, to help out those passengers (even with going to the restroom) without soliciting tips, and I didn't go a day without lifting something over 70 pounds. (Not to mention, I never received the $8.50 an hour I was promised when I started. Instead, I was put in a different position and knocked down from $8 to $6 an hour.) We each looked for other jobs, and I eventually found a better-paying position at a local vet clinic. My fiancé eventually found something at Blockbuster Video. It wasn't much, but we'd be slightly better off than we were ... or so I thought.

My new job took me three buses and a 2.5 mile walk to get there by 9 a.m. Needless to say, with the commute being about three hours (something that would have taken maybe 30 minutes by car if we'd had one), I had to leave home at 6 a.m., got off work at 6 p.m., and didn't make it back home until nearly 10 p.m. Even though I was traveling and not working for six hours of it, it was a 16-hour day for me: all the hassle of overtime without the pay. I never saw my fiancé, and never had the energy or time to do anything outside of work.

We were at our wits' end until a friend introduced us to a home business opportunity. His mentor explained how we could work from home and make a ton of money. Despite what we'd been through, my fiancé had a good relationship with his bank, and so we took out a $2,000 loan to get started. Meanwhile, my job informed me that they wanted me there at 6:15 a.m. instead of 9 a.m., which was utterly impossible due to the bus schedules, and I eventually had to quit. So here we were, with a $2,000 loan on our heads, and only one person working a job that paid about $7 an hour to maintain an apartment that was nearly $800 a month. But we had high hopes for the business, so we thought we would be okay.

Then it happened: we learned that the friend who had introduced us to the business opportunity was led astray by his mentor, and our $2,000 was gone! He had used it to get into the business, and all three of us were supposed to work together. But his mentor said that this wasn't allowed, and if we tried to be a part of it that he wouldn't help any of us. We had already paid, and the business was in the friend's name, leaving us in the dust. It ruined our friendship, and took us through a month of fighting back and forth to try to get the money back.

Though he did repay us, he did so in spurts; we got back $100 here, $300 there, which didn't help us to pay our bills. By the time it was all said and done, we were in debt with the bank, behind on rent, and on our last leg.

Thanksgiving was the killer, when my fiancé was told that he had to work or he'd lose his job. Because of everything we were going through, coupled with the fact that his pay didn't cover the bills anyway, he left his job and we spent Thanksgiving with our family. That Christmas was the worst one ever; we had to split up so that we could each move back in with our parents because we had no money and a *ton* of debt. I moved home to Georgia, to live with my sometimes-tyrant father, work seven days a week, and hope that I could save up enough money to get back to North Carolina.

But when the opportunity to start another business came up, I did things the right way. I raised my own money, studied like there was no tomorrow, and eventually earned enough to move back to North Carolina, where the man I loved was. I quit my job and by the grace of God was able to make a full-time income from home with my new business.

Today, I am nothing like that defeated person who hauled luggage bigger than I was and walked nearly three miles to get to work. I have a thriving business and I have gained respect in my community as a business leader.

That low point was truly a defining one, and I learned a *lot* of lessons. But the most important one was not to give up, ever! Even when the odds are thoroughly against you, you have to persevere. believe that people never quite know what they're made of until they're faced with such a situation, but now that I know, I will never go back to hoping without action. Action is the only thing that will pull you through and move you forward.

To those who have been through Hades on earth, remember that there is a Lioness in all of us. Sometimes it just needs to be awakened! Don't ever let go of that.

Hear Gillette Roar

It's only after you are out of it that you can see it. When you're in it, there is no perspective as your line of sight is consumed by the totality of the view in which you are living. This lack of perspective makes you believe that where you are is the only place you can be and that there is no possibility of something different. And this trap is not an uncommon phenomenon, as it seems almost everyone I know lives in their own version in one way or another, and in one form or another, at some point in their lives.

For me, I experienced this boxed existence for almost two years as a result of depression. At first, it wasn't obvious; it nibbled slowly, consuming a pixel at a time to use the parlance of our technological age, until I had lost all my color, all my verve and my ability to feel anything at all. I found myself at the bottom of a pit, realizing only too late that I had fallen into a rabbit hole too smooth to climb out of without some help.

But knowing you need help and having the energy to get it are two different things, so there I was, living 3000 miles away from home, crying or sleeping for close to 18 hours a day and getting by in the other six. And this went on for months and months. I was a house with all the lights on inside but not a soul rambling around giving the place a lived in and warm feel. I was a void. I felt nothing.

It was at the time when I realized and articulated that analogy to my best friend from whom I had been estranged for many months, that I had one of the most empowering moments of my life. It was the realization that despite that void and my absolute lack of care for myself, that I did know one thing for certain: that I would not commit suicide. I had thought about it, ways of going about it, and thoroughly considered the option of what it would be like to just not exist, and even craved to "just step off" the world for a little while so I could get myself collected. Yet there I was, making the one realization that actually proved to be my saving grace and the thing that actually formed the basis of my first step up and out of the rabbit hole.

The comfort of having that certainty about myself enabled me to recognize more things about myself, literally building one step at a time until I could see the light at the top of the hole which encouraged me even further, resulting in my head popping up out of the top where I could breathe and see the actual vistas and views of possibilities heretofore unbeknownst and inconceivable to me.

I still have days where I wake up to find I am at the bottom of that hole again. Normally I don't panic and fight it; I know that it is transient and that I will come out of it, that I in fact have the tools and self-knowledge to build that ladder again if I have to. That first step is permanently there, ensuring that no matter what, I can never get as low as that first time. And very much like a Zen proposition, the less I resist it, the quicker I am able build that ladder and get out of it.

It's been 15 years and despite the acute anguish that I felt and that I can recall only too easily now, I am just so grateful to have fallen into that first rabbit hole. Since then, I have come to distinguish some of the other traps in which I sometimes dwell, and to recognize them as being just that—traps that unnecessarily obstruct my vision of my life, of my dreams, and of the things that are important.

Hear Lee Ann Roar

Over the years I've learned a few things: wool sweaters shrink when washed in hot water; never eat and drive at the same time; opportunities sometimes appear in your life disguised as challenges that can surface like a shark to bite you in the butt until you recognize them for what they truly are.

Three years ago I had an idea: I was going to open a meal assembly kitchen that would be a fantastic success. Meal assembly kitchens were a new concept in the food industry; they were a place where customers came to assemble meals that would serve four to six people, using the kitchen's recipes and ingredients. Customers would then take those meals home to store in their freezers so that they would always have dinners on hand. For me, proof that the concept worked existed in a local franchise that was raking in almost a million dollars a year. I knew that with my culinary training I could create better food.

I found a location almost immediately and my store was open in less than two months. Five months later my business had almost reached its break-even point. I was close to making a profit—months before I had planned for that. I had a customer base of almost 150 loyal regular customers, great employees, and was beginning to feel like success was within my reach. I was busy and worked long days, but felt so fulfilled and happy it was worth it.

One morning, the phone shook me out of sleep about 2:30 a.m. It was the fire department. There was a store in the strip mall that my business was in that was burning (albeit under control). When I arrived on the scene, it was surreal. Smoke billowed from my store even though the nail salon that caught fire was two stores down. I sat in my car until the dawn broke through the haze. A man from a restoration company pressed a business card into my hands as he told me that his company could clean my store and was prepared to start immediately if I needed them.

I wasn't prepared for the stench when I was finally allowed to enter my store. The woman from the Board of Health ordered me to close until my shop could be thoroughly cleaned. All the food would have to be destroyed. I used that business card and the next day a crew appeared and cleaned my shop from the ceiling to the floor. When they were done I walked into my store, prepared to start anew, when it hit me: that stench. The store was clean, but it stank like an old campfire. I couldn't stay in my shop for more than a few minutes without choking. I was told I had to reopen anyway as it was just an odor and nothing that was harmful to food.

I knew I couldn't let my customers walk into my shop and experience that smell. How were they to stand the smell for the hour or two necessary to put their meals together? I fought back, calling in reps from my insurance company to experience first-hand the horrible lingering odor. Thankfully they came and agreed that my smoke damage was more extensive and so I remained closed. Weeks turned into months of my shop being cleaned again, treated with ozone and all types of apparatus to combat the stench — to no avail.

I made the decision to move, but I was out of money. My store manager, who I had come to know and trust, stepped up with some cash and became my 50 percent business partner. What I thought was a new beginning turned out to be the end. Within three months of buying in—for reasons I will probably never be privy to—my partner succeeded in destroying the very business she bought into. My business, my dream and $100,000 of my money: gone. Not only that, but I was being sued by four people because of it. I was forced to declare personal bankruptcy. And on the very day my bankruptcy was to discharge and I was to have a clean slate, my ex-business partner filed a lawsuit against me. I felt like Rocky Balboa being pummeled against the ropes by Apollo Creed.

That was over a year ago. Today, the case still hasn't come up for trial but I'm victorious regardless. I am not going to let a judge decide my fate. I not only forgive my ex-business partner for ruining my business and suing me, I thank her profusely for it. Because my experience with her and my failed business made me look at my life and see it in a way that I had never seen it before.

I invested in my own personal development and realized that I was responsible for the mess I was in — not circumstances, not my ex-partner, but me, myself and I. The day I realized that was the day I began my journey to personal freedom. No longer a victim, I had power; in fact, I had just as much power to create magic as mayhem in my life. I studied the spiritual laws of the Universe and pondered how they manifested in my life. I meditated and went deep inside to peel away layers of my false Self to reveal what was true about me.

And there in those murky depths of self-discovery, past the hurts of both my child and adult Self, past the fears of my ego, I am finding my true Self and making peace with the past. I'm discovering and uncovering my life purpose, which has something to do with writing and people of influence. I'm not totally clear on its true form yet but I will tell you this: just knowing that I have a purpose has set me free in ways that are truly magical.

I am now the author of a book about the mindset of women who make six figures and more on the Internet. The book is meant to empower women to the possibility that they can take what they have passion for and, by living in harmony with their life purpose, build a business and a lifestyle for themselves and their families. I am also being mentored to launch my own online business that will earn six figures or more in the next few years. Interviewing these ladies has made me realize that although I was passionate about my meal assembly kitchen, I was not in harmony with my life purpose.

I want you to know that wherever you are on your life journey it can be better. In fact if your mindset is right, it will be better. The best is always yet to come.

Lee Ann Price has been a Jackie of many trades: trained chef, radio producer, television talk show host, newspaper columnist, small business owner and author. Today, you can find her hanging with her son or working as the owner of a marketing consulting company. She believes that life is what you make of it and regularly blogs about the power of your mind to create the life of your dreams at www.leeannprice.com.

Chapter 4: Authenticity

***"Wherever you go, go with all your heart"*—Confucius**

In all our multi-talented, multi-tasking splendor, women sometimes feel pressured (whether real or imagined) to conform to others' norms and flex to others' wants and needs. This occurs regardless of a woman's dominant role in life, be it mother, spouse, professional, volunteer or all around "Superwoman." Here's an example from the corporate world: If a woman wants to join the executive ranks, should she learn to play golf even if she isn't really interested in the game, because she knows the golf course is where many male execs broker deals?

While there may not be any easy answers to these questions, the challenge for a woman to be herself and keep her own desires at the fore (pardon the pun) persists.

Interestingly, a corporate study conducted by RHR International concluded that women who succeed at the upper levels of business follow the same recipe as men (vision, intellect, hard work, courage) with one critical addition: authenticity. "Authentic Self" is also one of eight distinct attributes reflective of women's contributions to leadership, according to the ATHENA Leadership

Model®, developed through a grant from the W.K. Kellogg Foundation. So much for the argument that a female leader has to learn to play golf whether she likes the game or not.

Our Roar definition of authenticity is **being true to yourself, especially when it requires a willingness to defy conventional wisdom**. The seven women featured in this chapter made authentic choices — many of them career-related — that had a significant impact on their own lives and often on the lives of others. A good number of these stories almost ended up in the Generosity chapter — you'll see why when you read them. In all cases, these women are role models for daring to follow their hearts.

Meet Robin. When Robin learned she was pregnant, years after a devastating car accident that shattered her sense of self along with her pelvis, she knew she needed the support to carry and deliver her baby. "I was vulnerable and lacked confidence," Robin says. "I needed to feel nurtured, respected and honored through my pregnancy." Learn how Robin's unconventional decision to have a home birth with a midwife led to her personal renewal and inspired her commitment to help other pregnant women find their ability to roar.

Meet Mandy. Mandy's awakening came in the form of a major promotion that she had worked toward for years. Rather than being a cause for celebration, her achievement left her feeling unsettled, troubled, and ultimately very, very sick. Mandy writes, "My promotion was probably not the beginning of my unraveling, but it was the catalyst that forced my hand. It was the point at which I could no longer live with, or lie to, myself." Read about Mandy's subsequent leap of faith to find her calling.

Meet Lauren. Lauren is a highly educated professional woman who spent her 20's and 30's in high paying, high stress jobs. "By my mid-30's, I had accumulated several chronic pain conditions and had time for little else besides work and rest," says Lauren. At 38 and newly single, she chose to leave her job without another one in hand and move across the country. Read Lauren's story to learn how success can come from making a "downwardly mobile," risky choice.

Meet Natalie. Natalie describes herself as a late bloomer. At the age of 43 she left a corporate career in marketing to dedicate herself to her wardrobe consulting practice. "My old clients and colleagues cannot believe this is how I make money, and that I am really happy," says Natalie. When you read Natalie's description of her life just one year later, you will have a hard time imagining that this passionate and positive woman was once shy, withdrawn, and afraid to believe in her power.

Meet Yael. Yael's job as an Executive Banker didn't come easily. One of eight children raised by a single, drug-addicted mother, Yael was always determined not to become a statistic. But it wasn't until she left the banking business behind and opened her own Nanny Placement company that Yael began to realize her full power. Yael says, "Nannies allow mothers to return to work so that they, in turn, can provide for their families." Find out how Yael's commitment to living out her purpose in life is creating an empowering cycle for women everywhere.

Meet Cindy. Cindy spent 26 years in an unfulfilling relationship and a stagnant career in the family business. Cindy says, "Every time I wanted a career outside the family business, I was told 'There's a real world out there ... you won't make it.'" Then, at 45, Cindy gave up her so-called lavish life with very little money in her bank account and struck out on her own. Find out what riches awaited Cindy and her now-grown children, and why she no longer lets anyone tell her she cannot do something.

Meet Ginnie. Ginnie always knew she wanted to make some sort of mark as an artist in the world. Yet it wasn't until age 69, the year Ginnie had her first novel published, when the artist in her truly emerged. And that was just the beginning. Ginnie says, "I want every young woman to know there is no end to the road. Getting older just means you have time to achieve far more than you ever imagined." Read on to hear Ginnie roar.

Hear Robin Roar

Two weeks before Christmas, I was hit by a drunk driver and my world was turned upside down. Lying in my hospital bed, I felt helpless and scared. I had no idea what my recovery would be like or what my limitations would be.

The surgeon that pieced me back together was kind and compassionate as he told me I would no longer be able to walk on uneven surfaces. I was devastated — my career required hiking in rugged terrain. Besides the physical pain, I faced the pain of losing the career I had struggled so hard to obtain. My physical agility and strength were at the core of my identity. My sense of self was shattered. Although I survived the crash, a part of me died that tragic night.

For years, I believed the surgeon and did not even attempt to go hiking or rock climbing. I accepted an office job. I distrusted my body and believed I was weak. Then, I became pregnant.

Because of my lack of faith in my body, I wanted to have my baby in a hospital ... just in case. However, the hospitals in the town where I lived had recently dismissed all the midwives. A midwife supported me through my previous pregnancy and I knew I wanted and needed a midwife for the birth of this baby. I was vulnerable and lacked confidence. I needed to feel nurtured, respected and honored through my pregnancy and did not feel that would be available within the confines of the medical establishment.

Since being cared for by a midwife was not possible in the hospital, I decided to have a home birth. I sought out a midwife that was deeply spiritual, extremely experienced, and most of all loving and gentle. I am fortunate that I was able to find an incredible midwife that met all my criteria.

Throughout my pregnancy my midwife and I discussed my deepest fears. My pelvis had been fractured in the car crash and I worried that my body was not strong enough to carry my baby to full term or to give birth. My midwife listened to me with an open heart and spent as much time with me as I needed. I never felt rushed, patronized or judged. She believed in my innate wisdom and she believed in my body's ability to birth my baby.

As my baby and my belly grew, I started feeling healthier and stronger. I began to feel more confident and more trusting of my body's innate wisdom. By the end of my pregnancy, I believed that if my body could grow a strong healthy baby then it could certainly birth that baby.

The day after my due date, my water broke. I spent the good part of the day waiting for labor to begin. It was a perfect day — cool and sunny — so my husband and I decided to take a walk through our neighborhood. Many people were in their yards gardening and several commented about my huge belly. "When is that baby due?" and "Are you having twins?" they yelled. I answered confidently, "Our baby will be born today."

When we returned home we had a hearty dinner and then retreated to our room. We created a lovely space for the birth — with candles and flowers and a large birth tub that had been set up. The Buena Vista Social Club was playing on the radio, beckoning us to dance. My husband and I could not resist the call; we swayed with the music and sang along. I felt supported, loved, and ready to complete my baby's birth journey.

After some time dancing, I felt extremely tired. I needed to rest so I curled up in the comfort of my own bed with my husband by my side. About 20 minutes later, I was awakened by intense contractions. I told my husband to call our midwife. I knew we would meet our baby very soon. I began to hum and groan. The contractions became stronger and, for a moment, I doubted that I could do it. About then, my midwife arrived and suggested I move into the birthing tub. I resisted, but she gently and lovingly encouraged me.

I made my way to the tub, my husband's strong arms wrapped around me offering support. I slowly eased myself into the warm water, and my husband followed. He positioned himself behind me so that I could rest against him. The water felt wonderful. My midwife encouraged me to float in the water and not try to hold myself down. My enormous belly made my body buoyant and when I relaxed I simply floated. Beautiful chants played on the radio; I only occasionally noticed but found it comforting when I did.

The contractions were coming rapidly and were incredibly strong. I felt powerful; it was my strong body that was bringing my baby to me. During the height of my most intense contractions my husband asked me to kiss him. I must have looked at him like he was insane because he quietly said, "Trust me and kiss me." I kissed him and all the pain of the contraction melted away. I continued looking into his eyes and exchanging gentle kisses and within a very short time, felt the strong urge to push my baby out into the world. I told my midwife and she smiled and very gently said, "Okay."

I changed positions so I could relax against my husband between contractions. I began to bear down when my wise body told me it was time. After only a few pushes, my midwife said, "This time I need a really big push." I did not hold back; I let myself reach deep within and tapped into my primal instincts. I let out the most intense primal scream. As I roared, my baby moved from within my body into my waiting arms.

I was ecstatic! I held my sweet baby and showered kisses upon him. I had suspected he was a boy all along — again my instincts were correct. After a few moments of quiet, my midwife whispered, "That is a really big baby." I took another more focused look at my son and realized that, indeed, he was huge! When we weighed him we discovered he was 10 pounds! Not only did I birth him at home, but he was 10 pounds! I was so proud!

The birth of my son renewed my faith in my body and in me. That final push and loud roar helped heal the core of my spirit. Since his birth, I no longer believe I have physical limitations.

My son is now 4 years old and I take him for long hikes, walks about town, and I have plans to take him rock climbing. I am now a doula and childbirth educator. I share my experiences with other women hoping that it helps them find their ability to roar!

Robin Barbier is a certified doula, childbirth educator, musician and writer. With renewed confidence and vigor, she recently began working on her doctorate and plans to roar internationally as an advocate for children and families. Robin lives with her husband and two amazing children in the inspiring and bedewed Pacific Northwest.

Hear Mandy Roar

I am a white girl from the suburbs. I was raised to believe that the purpose of life is to climb the ladder. The *where* didn't matter; the point was the ascent. It would never have occurred to me, for instance, not to go to college right after high school. Or graduate school right after that. The question was not whether or not I wanted to do these things; climbing was just what you did.

From the day I joined Mercer HR Consulting, I began planning my progression along their particular ladder. Mercer was an entirely new universe to me. Human resources communication was new terrain as well. Nonetheless, I received my first promotion ahead of schedule, having been labeled "high potential." Then I set about to get the next one.

It took me four years to get that next coveted promotion. Mercer prides itself on allowing only the truly deserving to enter that realm. I crafted the compelling arguments my practice leader would need to present my case and I took on additional roles to ensure that my "numbers" would make that decision a no-brainer.

You'd think I would have been happy that day in late February 2005 when I learned that all my work had paid off. I cried, seemingly out of joy and appreciation for my practice leader's willingness to go to bat for me. But in retrospect, I believe that some part of me knew instantly that I was anything but happy.

My sense of unease set in almost immediately. At first I believed it was performance anxiety, then moved on to tell myself that I was just suffering from severe exhaustion. After all, I had been working superhuman hours for seven years.

Then I got sick. I love God's sense of humor. Naturally, I chose not to go to bed, but to my basement where I continued working, wrapped up in a blanket and voiceless (I love that part), intermittently crying, for over a week. So, here's the point in the story where I say that I looked up and realized that I was miserable on a variety of levels and that it was time to make some changes, right? I mean, sitting there hacking up a lung on client calls and working 12-hour days with a raging fever would shock anyone to their senses. I, however, prefer to push my capacity for self-abuse to extreme limits in order to learn life's lessons. Which is why it took one more ridiculous push from the Universe to send me over the edge.

The push came in the form of a phone call I received toward the end of my bizarre week in the basement, from a client manager I worked with who wanted to share with me his (and the client's) disappointment at the quality of work I had submitted earlier that week. Even I couldn't ignore the absurdity of that moment.

And so I fell.

First, I fell apart. I took a short vacation, but then I went back to work and continued to go through the motions. To my colleagues' credit, they gave me space during the next few months — to question myself and everyone around me, to cry at the drop of a hat, and to tell anyone who would listen that I had to get out.

But then I began to fall away from my fear. And things started to happen. I decided it was time to read "The Artist's Way," a book I had been dancing around for years. In an unanticipated moment of grace, I asked my friend Kelly to do the exercises in the book with me. In an equally gracious moment, she agreed. At the same time I began acupuncture. Through these two channels things started to shake loose. My chi moved. My imagination moved with it. I began to consider the possibility that I always have a choice. I like to believe that I literally started to change my mind.

I left Mercer. On the surface, the move wasn't dramatic. I simply went to another consulting firm, where I took on an internal role. I told myself it wasn't enough change. But then I gave myself permission to just make progress. Luckily, my new position was intolerable almost from day one. So I left corporate America altogether. I had absolutely no plan. I just quit, hoping that I'd be able to pick up some contracting work to tide me over while I became a rock star. I mean, how long could that take?

In another example of God's sense of humor, Kelly and I were scheduled to see our palm reader, Adrianne, the very evening that I knew I was leaving my new job. She explored the lines of my hand, talking about how I needed to go through a period of "horizontal growth" and how I could expect to be "at sea" — basically adrift with no clear picture of the future — for some time to come. And that is indeed how it was for some time. I had no idea where the money would come from, and I had absolutely no clue what I was doing; I just took it one day at a time.

I didn't become a rock star that year or the next. But I did find time to finish "The Artist's Way," write a slightly condensed version of my life's story, re-landscape my front yard, get to know my grandnephew, forge an amazing bond with Kelly, perform in several belly dance shows, choreograph and perform my first solo, discover the joy of daily walks, make my niece's wedding veil, begin writing song lyrics, take up singing lessons, meditate, live with a bit less fear, and a bunch of other stuff.

I still have no idea what I'm doing or where I'm going. But I'm pretty happy about the ride I'm on. And I have faith that, as I continue to allow at least a little room for horizontal growth, I will not be adrift forever. In the meantime, I have the privilege of being happy and of gardening during my conference calls from the privacy of my own yard.

Looking back, my promotion was the catalyst that forced my hand — the point at which I could no longer live with, or lie to, myself. What scares me now is seeing how hard I worked to keep up the illusion that I was happy about my choices; that I was on the right track. I knew, even then, that I had aspirations to find more creative or fulfilling work. But I told myself that was something for later, or for another life.

I'm reminded of three truths I hold near and dear: 1) Be careful what you ask for, since you will most likely get it; 2) Everything happens for a reason; and 3) Gifts come in all shapes and sizes and often in disguise. Most of all, this story is a poignant reminder of a universal truth I failed to remember at the time: usually, a door must close before another can open. That belief requires a leap of faith, I know. But where's the romance in life without a little faith?

Mandy Gordon is a communication consultant and facilitator by day and an aspiring songwriter by night. Her current project, "From the Ground Up," is a collection of songs, which she hopes to publish when the time is right. Until then, she continues to look for opportunities to blend her passions in ways that touch others for the better.

Hear Lauren Roar

I have chosen to share my story because I want to encourage other women to have the courage to look at their lives from many angles and realize that success can come from making a "downwardly mobile," risky choice — even if you are single and have to rely solely on yourself.

After obtaining my master's degree, I spent my 20's and 30's in high-paying, high-stress jobs working up to 90 hours a week. By my mid-30's, I had accumulated several chronic pain conditions, and had time for little else besides work and rest. Finally, at 38 and newly single again (thanks in part to long work hours and poor health), I made the rather risky decision to leave an incredibly demanding and unsatisfying director-level job with a West Coast based Fortune 500 — with no job in hand. I believed that another job would come, that I had the skills to find work when I was ready.

I was also struggling with my health, and the realization was strong that something in my lifestyle needed to change. I spent the summer at my parents' house in the Midwest, and did some soul searching. In the past, I had always measured my self worth by my monetary value, and I found myself compelled to search again for that high-powered job. After gathering some offers, I finally came to the realization that what I really wanted was a healthy life and time to enjoy it. That clarity came from recognizing that I am the only person who can live my life (I was no longer living for a man or a marriage, but for me), that that life, for me, was about quality, not material things, and that I had the fortitude to make this new life work for me. It was a rather scary prospect, but one that seemed to have potentially high payoffs.

Gathering strength from this new definition of self, I moved to the Washington, D.C., area (an area I handpicked for its social and cultural "extracurricular" opportunities) and networked until I found the right job for me. It had no fancy title or pay, but did have a great boss/mentor who believed in me and let me pursue my passion for career and leadership development within a top Federal agency. With regular hours and plenty of leave, this job allowed me the time to seek out new, empowering non-work activities that could also improve my health. For example, I learned how to rock climb, a challenge that gave me enormous satisfaction and made me realize my strengths — both mental and physical.

I am empowered by the meaningful work I'm doing, the life I have, and the active control I have over my finances, which allows me to live the life I want without relying blindly on a hefty paycheck. I'm also down to one intermittent pain condition, and life offers many possibilities. My relationships with my family and friends have been enriched by the healthier person I am today.

While I'm not a classic case of upwardly mobile success, I wouldn't change the "downward" course I have taken these past couple of years if I could. I have confirmed over time that the quality of my life now is much more rewarding than the quantity of things in my past. And that I can sustain this life on my own, with the encouragement of my loved ones.

Lauren Malmon (MA/HR) was promoted in her agency to a Career and Leadership management role and also has a thriving, new side business as a career coach (www.career-innovations.com). She finds time in her balanced schedule to volunteer for and speak regularly on career topics to a variety of national and D.C.-based organizations. Lauren can be reached at lauren@career-innovations.com.

Hear Natalie Roar

I am sharing my story because I believe it is inspirational and because I do believe I am a woman who can finally say, "I am woman, hear me roar!"

I was a young girl when that song was released but it always left an impression upon me. I guess deep down I always wanted to be able to believe those words for myself. But for so many years I lacked confidence. I was shy and withdrawn and simply afraid — of so many things, like doing the "wrong" thing, what others would think, not meeting the approval of someone important to me. I was afraid to take risks and to believe in my power, really.

I am a full-fledged late bloomer. I am 43 years young, and left a corporate career last August as a market researcher (same company for over 13 years!) to dedicate myself full-time to my wardrobe consulting practice. I started the business three years earlier (got trained and certified in the same year) and was building it on the side knowing that one day I would leave my career.

Well, I jumped ship, as they say, and the journey has been incredible. I am single (divorced) with no kids, have a mortgage to pay, yada yada, but I knew for awhile that I needed to start living my life on my own terms. Leaving my job was a *huge* step in that direction. It is tough as a woman-owned small business and I make so much less money than I used to, but I have *zero* regrets because I love what I do! And I am so proud of the woman I'm becoming!

Essentially I help women look and feel better because of their presentation of themselves via their clothing. I help empower and enrich women's lives and when you get that kind of career fulfillment the feeling is priceless. I love the people that are drawn into my life because of this process. And I know the money will come.

I am doing so many things as CEO of Elan Image Management. I help women shop, look great, de-clutter their closets, define their signature style, and look amazing. I help dress clients for special events. I conduct an image training workshop a few times a year to share my knowledge with would-be consultants. I give seminars to groups of women on various topics related to image and wardrobe. I participate in fashion shows as a stylist. And I am in the midst of forming a non-profit to serve women who cannot afford my services, while at the same time mentoring the many woman who contact me because they want to get in this field. The non-profit will give these women a place to practice their new skills and certainly see the fruits of their labor reflected in a satisfied client. And the clients will be working women who are living paycheck to paycheck and need the same boost of confidence and education as their peers earning more, but who do not have the discretionary income to do so.

My old colleagues and clients cannot believe this is how I make money and that I am really happy. A former client called me last week who thought I was still employed at my old company and he actually said, "Do people make money doing what you do?" I laughed because I understood the disbelief. To outsiders' eyes my decision to quit a corporate job was crazy. For me it was absolutely the best decision I could have made for my life and career satisfaction.

I have grown so much this past year as a woman, business owner and image coach. One of my most important priorities now is to leave a legacy. A legacy that others can look back on and say, Natalie Jobity stood for something and had an impact on the people she touched. I can feel that legacy unfold.

I am currently volunteering my expertise and time as the stylist for a local fashion event to benefit breast cancer charities in the Baltimore, Maryland area. The event, "Steps to the Cure," features models who are breast cancer survivors. The oldest is 70 years old! I am humbled and excited to participate in such an event as it is perfectly aligned with my mission to embolden and empower women. I get to work with a few of the designers in the show to help them design a gown for the model/survivor. And I get to work with these courageous survivors to ensure they look beautiful and like the stars of the event that they are. To hear their excitement and joy to have one night when they get to be those stars is so humbling. This is why I do what I do.

I am further validated that I am on the right path because people notice the difference in me. They say things like, "You seem really happy," or "You are so passionate about what you do," or "You are doing so well!" What they see is that spark, that twinkle in my eye, that fire in me that motivates and fuels me.

I attract different people in my life now too as a result. Cheerleaders instead of naysayers. Glass-half-full versus glass-half-empty folks. Positive people who have their own dreams, too.

It's wonderful to be in this place in my life. I am so blessed to be here. I am on the path, on the journey, and I can't wait to see where it will take me next. As the Jill Scott song says, "I am living my life like it is golden."

Natalie Jobity, wardrobe consultant and President of Élan Image Management, an image consulting firm, coaches women and men on how to look their best by helping them discover, define and project their own unique signature style and an image that positions them for success. Her business' motto, "Presence with a Purpose," is at the foundation of her vision for others. Visit her website at www.ElanImageManagement.com or e-mail her at Natalie@ElanImageManagement.com.

Hear Yael Roar

I have always been a giver. I am one of eight and I have always taken care to educate and advise my siblings. As the eldest, I was responsible for the daily care of my brothers and sisters. As adults, we still lean on each other for support.

Our parents separated when I was 7 years old, leaving my mother to care for eight very young children. She was very young and struggled to provide for us. We routinely had government support for housing and food, and I can remember moving at least six times while in grammar school because our landlords found out that there were nine people living in their apartment.

I hope to provide inspiration for anyone who has ever struggled.

I was not confident and I was insecure. My mother encouraged us to steal to support her habit and I knew that it was wrong and I was so conflicted by my guilt. My life goal as a teen was to not become a statistic. I did not want to be a teen parent and I never did drugs because I knew that drug abuse ran in my family and I wanted no part of it. My parents became incapable of caring for us when they were under the influence of drugs and I despised that effect. I always knew that I would not fall prey to the things that I saw as a child. Poverty, drug use and the despair that accompanies them were fodder for my dreams.

Rather than succumbing to my environment, I aspired to withstand and become strengthened by it. As a 20-year-old, I attended community college, not really sure of my pursuits but I knew enough that staying around people that shared similar goals would eventually take me where I needed to go.

I gained the friendship of a fellow student and I pursued employment at a local bank. From there I was promoted from teller to sales representative and then to executive banker. My experience allowed me to transfer within banks and I always obtained a position of good standing. I also met and married my spouse as a result of my banking experience. I was privileged to draw from the drive and ambition of my spouse. He aspires to be great and to provide well for his family. I stayed at home for six years to raise my children.

Then, after igniting the smoldering ashes that were my ambitions, I opened my Nanny Placement business to finally realize the whole power that I possess. I realized I could ultimately provide an income for myself and along the way empower other women to best use their experience and their talents to provide for other women to do the same. In effect, nannies allow mothers to return to work so that they can, in turn, provide for their families. This is an empowering cycle.

I am so fulfilled when I make a placement. I know that my purpose in life is to give of myself. Others become better when I am totally committed to making others and myself the best that we can be. I am now a confident, secure woman. I speak to children whenever I can — especially girls— because without support it is easy to settle for less. We have to help our girls realize their power, and to understand their greatness. We have to continue the cycle and give back to the power that has enabled us to get to where we are.

Hear Cindy Roar

I want other women to realize they have choices; they can be what they want.

Married at 19, I *thought* I made the right choice. In the 70's you generally got married right out of high school. I was married for 26 years and always felt that while I had material things, something was missing. I gave my life to my two wonderful kids, but dreaded them leaving and being left with "him." I worked with my ex. Every time I wanted or ventured into a career out of the family business, I was always told, "This is the best;" "You won't find a better job, career, or boss;" "There's a real world out there;" "You won't make it."

Others always said I had something special but I wasn't using it! At 45 I finally decided, "Enough!" I wanted to find what I was missing. So I gave up the so-called lavish life and, with very little in my bank account, got into a job that escalated my career, got a cute little "doll house," and began my new life. I gained strength and confidence. My personality came out. I came out of myself. I was on my *own*!

Shortly after, I found my soul mate, moved out of my "old" area, and started a new life. My husband and I have been together for six years, married for over three years of that. I truly did marry my best friend, and he's a huge supporter in all aspects. I learned that you can love someone but being *in love* is completely different; it's the missing ingredient that brings it all together!

Now I have a wonderful life, but on a *realer, healthier, happier* level. My grown kids now realize the difference. They see that you can have what you want, and it doesn't always hinge on money. Money is not everything; it will not truly make you happy. A lavish house means nothing if it's not a home!

I no longer let anyone tell me I cannot do something. If you want it, go for it! You may bust your butt doing it, but in the end you feel so damned great! Don't let others control you or create your happiness; do it yourself.

Also, never consider something as a failure or a mistake. It's a learning experience. Sometimes it's due to the decisions made at the time, with the information available.

Be happy, be in love, build your dream! Dare to make changes! ENJOY LIFE!

Cindy Colucci resides in Old Bridge, New Jersey with her wonderfully supportive husband, Dean and her new puppy, Logan. She has a successful home-based business with Arbonne International. Her philosophy is to help others realize they do have choices and to achieve their wildest dreams. She believes strongly in "DREAM...BELIEVE.... ACHIEVE! What you think about, you bring about." Cindy can be contacted at cindycolucci@myarbonne.com and www.cindycolucci.myarbonne.com.

Hear Ginnie Roar

At the age of 42, at 2 p.m. on a Sunday afternoon, I had one of those a-ha! Moments: *I don't want to spend the rest of my life like this.*

That was the push off the starting line, although I sure didn't know it at the time, I just sat down at my kitchen table and spilled my guts about how I felt at that moment. Fast forward to age 69, when I had my first novel published. And then take another leap to 2008, when I celebrated my 77th birthday on a movie set where Hallmark Theater was filming a TV movie based on that novel.

I want every young woman to know that there is no end to the road. Getting older just means you have the time to achieve far more than you ever imagined. Today I am a publisher, a writer and very happy woman!! Here's the story of my amazing trip to Hollywood. On an ordinary Wednesday morning I find myself standing in my shower wondering what I should wear to Jane's funeral. Now that's weird. There isn't any Jane that I know of, other than the ill-fated woman I wrote about nine years ago.

Sometimes writing a book is a carefully planned, thoughtfully plotted, neatly organized endeavor. Other times (ask any writer) it's a willy-nilly, "I wonder what's coming next" sort of thing. That's the way it was with this novel. Totally willy-nilly. One night, on a whim, I keyed in the first few sentences on the computer. Liked how it sounded so I just kept on writing. And then in the first paragraph, Jane shows up. "Dear-old-anything-but-plain Jane" says the yet-to-be-named narrator.

By the end of the first chapter Jane has announced her reason for coming to visit. She is going to die, and she needs to say goodbye to her best friend, Ida Mae, and the life she left behind many years before. Nobody is more surprised by this announcement than I am. I'm just playing... conjuring up a pretty scene between two friends. No plot intended.

I finish the chapter, and go to bed wondering where this turn of events will take me now. After that, Jane and Ida Mae consume my life. Days I rush through my work mindlessly, the gotta-get-it-done-today stuff so that I can get to the real work: writing the story. The scenes unfold on the monitor before me; the characters reveal themselves to me through the pages of Ida Mae's diary.

Nights are filled with a tumble of sentences. The title appears: "Ida Mae Tutweiler and the Traveling Tea Party." Hmmmm. Wonder how I'm going to explain a traveling tea party. I haven't a clue. Funny thing is, the late night imaginings stay in place. Crisp and clear in my mind for the next day's work. What fun!

And then it's finished. I'm tired and empty. It's been exciting. I've been writing for a long time, but this time is different. I really like what I've done. Then the miracle begins ... unexpected and certainly unforeseen. The book gets published, and a friend sends it to a screenwriter he knows. Finally, a mere eight years later the script gets into the hands of a producer at Hallmark.

The rest is history. Contracts all around, I get a screen credit and a nice check and plan a trip to Hollywood. And the producers say, "Sure, you're welcome to come watch the filming. We'd love to meet you!" Wow. It's May, my birthday month, and we are going to be there on my 77th birthday. On the very day I celebrate my birth all those years ago I'm going to be there to watch the filming of my book. It's now being called "The Glass Seagull" (at least temporarily). Wow again.

We drive to a remote ranch deep in the desert mountains of Simi Valley. The "studio" is at the end of a 15-mile long rocky and rutted dirt road. Finally we arrive, lots of cars and big trailers parked in neat rows. I am overwhelmed. It crashes over me like a big wave: they are here because of what I did one night. All of this is because *I wrote that book.* I see it and I hear it, but I can't get my head around it.

We are bussed up a steep hill to an old Victorian style house, long porch wrapped all around the outside, and cameras, sound booms and lights the size of a small car and people swarming around everywhere. The house, we are told, is the one used in the TV series "Little House on the Prairie" —how neat is that?

We are graciously welcomed, offered cold water and instructed to sit on the back part of the porch and stay quiet when they yell, "Quiet!" When I am introduced to anyone, it's always as "the author" which is greeted with warm enthusiasm. I'm having a ball. The director puts us in the kitchen scene. We shoot the scene two or three times, I really can't remember.

Then it happens. The high point of my life. The director yells from the living room, "Get Gin in here, I want her in here!" Holy smoke! He's going to put me in another scene! I float in on a little cloud, and then, the next thing I know someone is standing in front of me with a huge cake. On the top is a picture of the cover of my novel in frosting and below the picture it says, "Happy Birthday Ginnie." The whole cast and crew sing "Happy Birthday" to me.

Well, of course I cried. You'd have to be made of granite not to cry at a thing like that. I know we drove back home , and I guess it took as long as it did to get there, but I honestly can't say...I was in a trance, the sound of those people singing to me still ringing in my ears.

When I was a child, I wanted to grow up and be somebody, to make some sort of my own mark as an artist in the world. Then reality showed up on my doorstep, and informed me that my mark was to be a wife and a mother. I did the wife part far less than perfectly, although I'm happy to say I have five wonderful children and no mother is prouder of her kids and their kids than I am.

And now, at long last, the artist has made her mark as well. In the grand scheme it's only a teeny mark, but it's there. And before it's over, a million or more people will see what began in my head that night nine years ago. I'm a writer, it's true, but I don't have the words to express how good that feels.

Chapter 5: Faith

"The smallest seed of faith is better than the largest fruit of happiness" **— Henry David Thoreau**

Women are often celebrated for our strength, resourcefulness and grace. When faced with challenges, struggles, road blocks and dark times, we dig deep and tap into our well of resources to find something — anything — to help us cross the abyss and shed light on the next action to take. Sometimes this requires us to believe in something for which there is no tangible proof or rational explanation, otherwise known as ... faith.

We've defined faith as **placing deep trust in yourself or something larger than you**. For some of the seven Roar authors featured in this chapter, faith is tied to believing in themselves — their own innate wisdom or "center." For others, it is about God. For others still, faith stems from a more amorphous divine, benevolent presence, a connectedness to spirit, a higher self. In all cases, these women created powerful partnerships with inspiring results.

Meet Kelly. One rainy April morning, Kelly had a car accident that jolted her physically, emotionally and spiritually. She had just turned 40 and fled an abusive relationship. She was flat broke, without income, and homeless. Kelly says, "I needed to get back to my "center" — a place of inner wisdom, balance, purpose and strength." Find out what basic tools Kelly found and employed as her anchors during the next five years of steady, grounded, gradual climb up and out of the hole she dug for herself.

Meet Sheila. Sheila, a cantor for 20 years, got unexpected news from her temple president one cold February night: her contract would not be renewed. She was 62 and caring for her husband who was dying of a terminal illness. Sheila says, "I was being challenged to dig deep and find my greatest source of power and energy: my own inner wisdom, my own inner strength, and my own inner resilience." Learn about how Sheila tapped into her intuition, vision and courage in the face of this personal crisis to discover what she was born to do.

Meet Ellen. Growing up with a mentally ill and abusive mother, Ellen describes a childhood rife with fear, out of which she found a source of love that she thought would never hurt or abandon her — food. Ellen writes, "It was the perfect balm for the fear, a powerful dam to hold back all the feelings and the ultimate numbing agent for me." Find out how Ellen's emerging belief in her Higher Power — her core of truth and self-love — has played a critical role in her recovery.

Meet Janis. Janis describes meeting a retired nurse from Arizona named Rose as a pivotal moment in her life. Janis says, "Rose taught me a practice that I felt ignite within me and open deep channels that have been purifying and healing me ever since." Find out how Janis now stays connected with "the hugeness of all that is."

Meet Emily. Pregnant and married at 17, Emily has given her life to raising her three daughters. Her second was diagnosed with cancer as a child, then later paralyzed from the waist down after 12 years in remission — shortly after Emily's third daughter was born. Emily says, "All I could do was pray that God would give me the strength to see me through." Read Emily's story to find out why she believes God led her down the road less traveled.

Meet Maimah. Maimah was diagnosed with aggressive Stage 2 breast cancer at the age of 32. Within three months, she was bald, sick from chemotherapy, and terrified of leaving her 3-year-old daughter without a mom. She writes, "Finding myself in a very desolate place, I prayed to God to restore my spirit." Read Maimah's story to find out how God answered her prayer.

Meet Rita. Rita hit the skids and crashed at the age of 50, falling into a deep depression that lasted more than a year. On a routine visit to her internist, he suggested a therapist who, it turned out, was very spiritual. "Early on she told me I needed a spiritual element in my life but I had no idea what she was talking about," Rita writes. Find out how Rita's "Dearest Divine" has since helped her transform her life.

Hear Kelly Roar

It started with a car accident and a broken heart.

I had just turned 40 and fled an abusive relationship. I was flat broke, without income and homeless. On that cold rainy April morning, it all came to a head as I plowed into the back of the car in front of me.

Pulled off to the roadside, huddled in my borrowed car, I sobbed and waited while the police finished at the scene. Out of nowhere, a woman with a warm smile knocked on my car window and handed me an even warmer mug of steaming chai tea. She said, "Looks like you're having a bad day. Here, maybe this will help." Stunned, I gratefully accepted her offer and she disappeared into the gray day.

Flashback five years earlier to a marriage in shambles, premature menopause, a failing dot-com venture, looming financial disaster and a strained business partner relationship. Life in my 30's was not going as I had expected. Why was this happening and why did I keep finding myself back in this place, only to rise again, like a determined phoenix from the ashes? What was I doing to sabotage my success, time after time?

After canceling the rest of my appointments on that dreary day, I returned to my sister's home where I was temporarily living, downed two sleeping pills and disappeared into my room for the next 24 hours. Somewhere at about hour 15, a very clear thought emerged from my pathetic haze: I can choose not to live this way anymore. I can choose not to play the victim. I can make better choices.

That was it. I decided right then and there that there would be no more crises, no more drama, no more bailouts from family and friends, no more helplessness, no more unaccountability for the messes I had created. Most importantly, I needed to get back to my "center" — a place of inner wisdom, balance, purpose, and strength.

As a lifelong ballet dancer, I had experienced this literally and figuratively. When I looked back on the pattern of successes and failures, they had one thing in common: paying attention (or not) to my inner wisdom, my heart, my intuition, my knowing — feet on the ground — my center. When I ignored it ("Sure, let's leave our well-paying day job and invest 100% of our time and money in a sexy new dot-com venture — why not? Everyone's doing it and they love us!"), I paid a high price. When I listened to it ("Go back to graduate school — you are smart enough — the money will follow"), I thrived.

The more I thought about it, the more I realized that reconnecting with — and never losing sight again — of my center was key to my long term wellbeing. It was a moment of complete clarity and a turning point in my life. When the clouds cleared after that dark day, it was like a light turned back on inside of me.

The next five years have been a steady, grounded gradual climb up and out of the hole I'd dug for myself. Since then, I've established a stable and viable business, met and married the right man, have come out of denial about the effects of addiction and co-dependence in my family of origin, have acknowledged that work and "busyness" are my drugs of choice, and have reclaimed the artist in me. As I turned 45 this year, I've come to appreciate that "easy really does get it done." Not that any of this has been easy ... but I seem to have found some basic tools that are working for me, including therapy, acupuncture, a daily ritual of yoga/meditation/journaling/walking, art and a few well-chosen friends. These, along with my husband, are my anchors.

It's wonderful to discover how doing less, slowing down and making good choices garner good things that I could not even have imagined five years ago. Sure, I still stumble into holes instead of walk around. And while I try to not jump into them intentionally, it happens. The difference now is that the downward spiral does not pick up a head of steam to derail me. My antennae are more sensitive and I take measures to course-correct or recover more quickly. My choices are more conscious and I'm slowly falling back in love with the parts of me I'd learned to not tolerate a long time ago.

My heart is on the mend. I've started to forgive myself, grieve the losses and feel compassion for those who have hurt me. And I finally feel ready to be there for others, now that I'm doing a better job at caring for myself.

Kelly O'Brien is a change management consultant for the federal government, while she hatches plans for a transition into the arts fulltime. Through the book arts, she continues to tell her story. You can reach her through her blog, Designing a Life, at http://www.turningpointepress.com/blog.

Hear Sheila Roar

It was a dark and cold February night; the phone rang and it was the temple president calling me. "Cantor Pearl, I'm calling to inform you that the Board of Trustees has voted not to renew your contract." Silence.

I was stunned and Jerry wasn't saying anything more. What? What in the world is he talking about? No one had spoken to me about a question of renewing my contract; we were going to discuss an increase in salary at this point in time. Instead, I get a call telling me I'm done, as of June. Wow!

For over 20 years, I had been serving congregations as a cantor. I had been with this congregation as both cantor and educator for five years. People had expressed that I was "the best thing that ever happened to us!" And I get this call! I was 62 years old and my husband was home with me, dying of a terminal illness. I was certainly in no position to seek another congregation, to put myself and husband through the stress of uprooting ourselves and moving. What to do?

I had been planning for my next career: to have a full-time life coaching practice. I was just afraid of being totally on my own, self-supporting, in a field many people still didn't know anything about. How could I sustain myself and generate the kind of income necessary to care for my ailing husband? I was being challenged to dig deep and find my greatest source of power and energy: my own inner wisdom, my own inner strength, and my own inner resilience, in the face of abject terror.

A couple of days after this shocking call, while I was still dizzy from the shock and dismay I was feeling, I called a congregant in the real estate business. I asked if he knew of office space that would be available to me. He said "Yes, come with me. I have the perfect space for you!"

Sure enough, there it was: my perfect space. Like a big living room, with high ceilings and tall windows, I could see my perfect office in my mind's eye. I called some friends for support.

Without even asking, some loaned me money so that I would have the capital to set up my practice. I advertised. I joined networking breakfast and dinner clubs. I offered free classes and coaching sessions. Quickly my practice started to grow. I was doing whatever it took to make it thrive.

It's now four years later. I bless my congregation for releasing me! I began to understand more about how I had contributed to their feeling that we were no longer a "good match" for one another. They were accurate: we were not. They were also releasing me to be and do what I had been planning to be and do, anyway.

At the age of 66, now a widow, my life-coaching practice is thriving. I am free to be "out of the box" and to grow personally and professionally in ways I couldn't even dream about! I have authored two books and co-authored two others, with many books in me yet to be born. I have recently launched a public-speaking career, as well — something I was born to do.

I want others to hear my story, as a reminder that it is truly never too late to launch a new career, to pick yourself up and triumph in the face of disappointment and challenges, and that the very thing that you initially thought was a terrible thing could — and usually does — turn out to be our greatest blessing and gift!

Being employed by a congregation as a clergy person can be very rewarding; it can also be very restrictive. For me, I was often feeling constrained and tethered by being tied to a congregation. Now, I love to be free and to set my own schedule. I also love to serve people of all walks of life and religious/spiritual persuasions. And because I was able to eventually bless my congregation for what they chose to do, we have remained friends and I am still in the same community, often attending services and events as their special guest.

My community has simply expanded. And so has my heart.

Hear Ellen Roar

When Harry Potter had to recall his happiest childhood memory in order to conjure a protective spirit to help him fight off his greatest fear, he struggled to come up with a memory strong enough and happy enough to produce an embodied spirit. Looking back, I see that none of my childhood memories had a fraction of the joy and spirit that the soul of a child should feel.

All of my memories conjure up fear and it's that feeling that guided my life. Fear of being abused by a mother who was severely damaged mentally and devoid of most human and humane responses. Fear of never finding a way to appease her and her rage and her relentless pursuit to destroy the lives of those around her — lives she created.

But I found a source of love that I thought would never hurt me or abandon me — it was food. In the largest quantities I could obtain and as often as possible. It was the perfect balm for the fear, a powerful dam to hold back all feelings and the ultimate numbing agent for me. And then the food created a physical barrier, an insulator from the world that produced enough fat to store the pain and fear and would encompass my body and buffer everything. Like a flak jacket or a bullet proof vest.

The irony is that I lived and tried to thrive under the delusion that if I was funny enough, talked quickly enough and was charming enough people wouldn't notice the weight. It only reinforced my absolute belief that I was not lovable and would never be enough and that there was never enough food to make me forget that.

But I was blessed with other people in my life who helped me feel that I could make a life. I married a man who truly loves me and I gave birth to a wonderful, magical daughter. My constant companion, however, was still food and morbid obesity was an inescapable physical manifestation of all that I carried around.

I made many attempts to lose the weight, not realizing that unless and until I didn't need it anymore, it would only come back and in greater numbers. I also wasn't aware of three crucial facts:

First: Food is not the problem. It's a symptom of a disease — compulsive overeating.

Second: I'm not alone. There are people out there like me. People who have a relationship with food that's unlike anything a "normal" person could comprehend. A relationship that is a complex and powerful combination of love and hate. And, like me, many felt like they could never escape and find recovery.

Third: That there's a power greater than myself that gives me the courage and strength to reveal, heal and live a life of recovery; that food doesn't have any power over me if I hold onto this belief. It's my higher self — my core of truth and self-love that's willing to embrace all that I am and the journey that brought me here. A power that will guide my way when I don't feel like I can move forward, when I want to believe that food is the answer.

I discovered all of this and much more through Overeaters Anonymous — a 12-step program that saves countless numbers of lives one day at a time. Today I work on healing all aspects of my life by living a life of sobriety that includes a food plan that helps me nurture my body—not using food as a weapon that erodes my physical, emotional and spiritual health and robs me of my ability to be in the moment without the need for a buffer. I'm grateful for the release of weight from my body and know that it happens when and because I believe I don't need it.

The number of pounds is daunting and unimaginable to most people but I have faith in this program and my recovery. I do my part by acknowledging what's happened and honoring all that brought me here — good and bad — and let those lessons become part of the life force that guides me to a happier, more fulfilling and nurturing future.

By honoring the defense mechanisms and protective responses that I developed as a result of my past, I now realize that divine guidance was at work in my life at all times. The little girl who hoped and prayed that the abuse would stop is now the woman who has an abundance of hope for herself, her family and fellow food addicts and compulsive overeaters.

I now pray, not out of desperation, but with the heartfelt and absolute belief that we all possess a divine grace that will guide us. I believe that my Higher Power can't prevent bad things from happening but that I'll always be given what I need to get through the worst of times if I reach out and stay in grace. By living and believing that I'm not alone unless I choose to be. I'm learning to celebrate the little girl who felt guilty because she could charm people and make them like her because I realize it wasn't selfish manipulation but a gift. It's a gift that allows me to show kindness, compassion, humor and love in an authentic way. I'm grateful for being able to think quickly and communicate effectively, not as the fast talker that just needed to be heard, but as a woman who's respected for her insights and intellect.

I've also learned that listening empowers us because we all want to be heard and have someone know that we are here. I was always the kid who laughed too much and too nervously but I've come to rely on my ability to laugh easily and find humor in life and I willingly share it with others. And it's not a frantic, fearful or diversionary tactic. I'm easily amused and I laugh at my own jokes—what a blessing! It just feels good and that's recovery.

Recovery is also dealing with shame and realizing the importance of forgiveness. Forgiving my abusers for what they did knowingly or because of their own illnesses and addictions and, most importantly, about forgiving myself. To let go of the self-loathing and shame about my body, my life and my disease and much, much more. I'm learning to be gentle with myself and realize that I was doing what I could with what I had and in the only way I knew how.

I know now that I matter and that I'm worthy of love and all that comes with it. I know that I'm in recovery and in grace each day that I believe that. I attend and lead meetings, do service and sponsor others. I'm profoundly grateful to know that I'm blessed and that's why I'm telling my story. So no one has to believe they are alone with any addiction, compulsion or life limiting fear.

Reaching out blindly is frightening but reaching out with the belief that I'm not alone and that my story may help someone else is what my life is about now.

Ellen lives in Maryland with her husband and teenage daughter. She's grateful for the gift of recovery that she receives one day at a time and the support she receives from her family and friends. You can reach Ellen at gratefulcoe@comcast.net.

Hear Janis Roar

We live in a society that glamorizes youth, and women as well as men face pressure to mask signs of aging. Whatever form of falseness you choose to invest in — Botox, breast implants, liposuction, hair dye and more — it is all available at market rates. But if you paid me 10 million dollars, I would not want to live my youth over again.

For me the time I shook hands with my own power began after 30, when I met a retired nurse from Arizona named Rose, and began a journey that is awakening me to my soul's purpose and the reason I was born.

I would never claim to be awake, like some enlightened beings, self realized masters of various spiritual lineages who have completely actualized their human potential through their practice —Jesus, for example, or Buddha, or Sri Aurobindo, or Swami Sivananda — to name only a few great avatars who have appeared at times of humanity's great need to teach, to serve, to heal. But before I met Rose and practiced yoga for the first time, I was in the wilderness in my life, alone in darkness and unconnected with a great ideal to serve.

In all the material abundance of my Canadian upbringing and surroundings of the 60's, 70's and 80's, I was in despair beneath a patina of social cheerfulness, for my life felt purposeless and empty. I had dreams of darkness, yet more than dreams, for when I woke up the darkness was still there, imbuing my life, distancing me from everyone with apathy and exhaustion, although on the surface I seemed to be doing all the right things — running laps, running marathons, winning prizes, graduating from university, working. I dreamed of falling into dark pits, unable to climb out, of watching my own face being eaten alive by ants, of drowning, snagged on underwater trees, of being shot through closed doors and watching my own blood spatter the blue kitchen wall behind me.

Each night as I prepared to sleep I prayed I would not have those dreams, but the other ones that sometimes came, the dreams of liberation, of flying over colourful carpets of autumn forest, over blue water lapping white towns, my body immediately responsive to my thoughts to float up cliffs effortlessly, and to hover and dart at will.

Rose by no means rescued me, but taught me a practice that I felt ignite within me and open deep channels that have been purifying and healing me ever since. Every morning at the meditation retreat I had joined, she led us in a yoga class, and in these ancient postures, the twists, the inversions, the forward bends and back bends, and the corpse position of perfect stillness, I experienced a quality within me I have never known in any other life experience I have since encountered. I knew this was my practice. I knew this was my way home. Without doubt, fear or question I felt yoga resonate within me and I knew this was the most priceless of pearls, this was what I had come into the great bazaar of life to find, to remember, to embody.

I have had moments of transcendence in life, like on the cliffside in northern Scotland above Achiltibuie overlooking the Summer Isles and Ullapool, when the mist swirled beneath my feet, the sheep bleated above me on the mountainside while the sea petrels cried below me as they soared on the wind and sought fish to dive for. In the stillness after days of near-fasting and silent meditation, I felt my energy open near the base of my belly and suddenly I expanded. For some timeless period I was the wind, I was the mountain, I was the light of the gleaming sea and the blackness of the Summer Isles silhouetted on the shining path of the sun. I was huge, eternal, and Real.

For me yoga is a discipline which offers a path to what is real. In the face of life's vicissitudes and all the suffering each human life encompasses, yoga gives a way to stay connected with the hugeness of all that is. Of course it is not really a path back, for in fact we have never been separated — only our minds and the barriers of our own ego make us believe we are separate, that we are our bodies, our names, our social personality, our job or role in life, our money, our vacations, our hair colour, our physical youth or beauty. But yoga teaches us that what is real is not any of these things. These things of time and change, of beginnings and ends are "asat," unreal, and only the things that were never born and never began and will never end are real —

the stuff of spirit, or "brahman" in the vocabulary of advaita philosophy which yoga comes from.

As my practice matures and deepens, once impossible postures become easy, my focus shifts to cultivating the inner qualities of yoga, and I begin to understand that the more I learn about this infinite practice, the more I know nothing. Along the way I have become a teacher and to my amazement students look to me as if I have something to teach them. Compassion, discrimination, non-attachment, non-violence, recognizing one Self in all that is, these are the real lessons yoga offers humanity.

Our teachers are all around us—not only on the yoga mat, but off, in our fears, our perceived threats, in the angry bosses, the bad-news bankers, the crying children, the enraged drivers who cut us off in traffic. Shaking hands with our own power is something that we can only do for ourselves, for the only power there is, lies within us. It is not in money or fame or beauty or any form of empire we may choose to establish.

As I stand now on the final side of menopause and feel the liberation that brings, I remember old dreams of flying and know I am living them now. I watch my daughter move into the circle of life as I step back from it; I see the generations pass. I share this now in the wish that every daughter in the world, and every son too, might find the way to experience this for themselves.

The best part of yoga for me is the feeling of joy it has brought to my life, the deep sense of purpose and knowing that even if I die tomorrow, it won't matter, that I will have done my part to keep the teachings alive for humanity, and that others will continue to carry on the work.

Janis Goad is a yoga teacher and Reiki practitioner. She writes about holistic healing and speaks at conferences about managing stress with yoga and meditation. She has produced a series of yoga and relaxation DVDs available now at http://www.merumountainyoga.com and soon through Living Spectrum Holistics at http://www.janisgoad. com.

Hear Emily Roar

I am Emily Hinson.

I have chosen to share my story because I feel that if I can overcome the many things in life that have been thrown at me, then others can overcome whatever they are going through.

I met my husband when I was a sophomore in high school. We dated throughout school and at the end of my junior year I became pregnant with my first daughter, Chelsea, who is 17. Once we found out that I was pregnant we got married and have been married for 18 years.

Being a mom at such a young age was not easy. I had to give up my life as I knew it to care for another life. After several years we decided to have another child, Savanah, now 15 years old. Life was great! The perfect family; a wonderful husband, two beautiful girls and living life to the fullest.

May 24, 1994, was a day I will never forget. After Savanah fell one day while having pictures taken and bumped her head, she had difficulty for weeks using her legs. On that day, doctors told me that my daughter had cancer.

For two years she was in and out of the hospital for surgeries, chemotherapy, infections, and sickness. For those two years, I was pulled between caring for my two children. Knowing Savanah needed me with her at the hospital and required all my attention there, and Chelsea needed me at home to just be her mommy.

It was very difficult for me to balance my time so that I could meet each of their needs. In April 1996, doctors considered Savanah cancer-free, which she has been for the past 12 years.

Life returned to normal and we moved on with our lives. I decided to go back to college and pursue a degree in elementary education. This meant that I would have to work during the day and go to school at night. For eight years I did this. During my last year of college, my life again changed.

In July 2006 I found out that I was pregnant. This was unexpected as I had not planned on having any more children. Again, our life changed from how we once knew it. It had been 13 years since I had dealt with a baby in my life and I had to readjust how I did things. But the good Lord took care of me once again.

As if adding a new child to the mix wasn't hard enough, Savanah started having complications with her back due to the surgeries she had had as a baby to remove the tumor in her back. After seeing several doctors, she was diagnosed as having kyphosis, the forward curvature of the spine, and scoliosis, the sideways curve of the spine. Since the kyphosis was so severe, she required surgery to place rods and screws along her spine to help with the problem.

Unfortunately, the surgery did not go as planned. As a result, she is now paralyzed from the waist down. Just like when she was diagnosed as a baby with cancer, my time was now redirected to her again to help with her disability. I struggled now with spreading my time among not only two daughters, but three. My whole life was turned upside down. How was I going to care for a baby and a daughter in a wheelchair?

All I could do was pray that God would give me the strength to see me through. Over the last year God has made me a stronger person because of the paths I have been down.

I am reminded of the poem by Robert Frost about the two roads. God led me down the one less traveled, because He knew that I would have the faith to get through the trials I have been dealt throughout my life. I am not saying it has been easy, but I am saying that it can be done. My best friend and I had a motto that got us through school which was, "You do what you gotta do!" I still stick to this motto.

If I had let all the troubles in my life get me down, then I would not have been able to move forward and accomplish all the things I have. My self-confidence is so much greater knowing I have overcome the many obstacles I have been dealt.

When others see me they always ask me how I do what I do. I just tell them it is because of God that I have made it through everything.

Emily Hinson lives in Salisbury, NC. She is an elementary teacher and mother of three beautiful girls. Emily plans to write a book in the future about the many blessings God has bestowed upon her family. Emily can be reached at emily_hinson@yahoo.com.

Hear Maimah Roar

On February 28, 2006, I received a call no woman ever wants to get. The voice on the other end said, "You have breast cancer."

I was 32 years old and the mother of a 3-year old. I was finally at a place in life where I was getting ready to exhale and enjoy the fruits of my labor. I had fled to the United States with my family when I was 16 and had worked hard to build my life to where it was. In a matter of months after my diagnosis, I watched my life fall apart.

I had aggressive Stage 2 breast cancer. I was told that I had to have surgery, chemotherapy and radiation. Within three months, I found myself bald, sick from chemotherapy and wondering what in the world had happened to my life and what would become of my dreams. I was terrified of leaving my daughter without a mom.

During my second round of chemotherapy, I realized that I needed to do something to make an impact on this disease. There were few well-known resources that targeted women under 40 as it pertained to breast cancer and made them aware of the risks. Furthermore, young women faced more isolation and unknowns; although there are fewer of us getting breast cancer under 40, we have more aggressive forms of breast cancer and higher mortality rates.

Finding myself in a very desolate place, I prayed to God to restore my spirit. I didn't know how long I would live, but I just wanted to be myself again and I wanted to use my life in some way. I promised that if He restored me, I would use my life for His service.

The next morning, I felt like I had been cleansed and my spirit was more alive than it had ever been. He had touched me! Soon, I began to get ideas to form an organization called Tigerlily Foundation, a breast cancer foundation to educate, advocate, empower and support young women affected by breast cancer.

Today, Tigerlily Foundation (www.tigerlilyfoundation.org) is helping women around the world. We provide education to young women; we provide chemotherapy buddy support, financial support, empowerment, free mammograms and other services.

Lives are being saved because more young women are being encouraged to use their voices to spread the word. My dream is that young women will become vigilant self advocates and as a result, we will lower the mortality rates of young women from this disease. Death is preventable if a woman is diagnosed in time. I encourage women around the world to join Tigerlily Foundation as advocates, as volunteers and as a source of empowerment to others.

When I was diagnosed, I thought my life was ending; little did I know that it was only the beginning. God is amazing. Through Him *anything* is possible. When I face a challenge now or see one coming, I embrace that challenge because I know that it is His way of strengthening and molding us to be a source of empowerment and catalysts for change in others' lives.

I am very thankful for the experience of breast cancer in my life. I am thankful that it has propelled the real me to show up in my life, as a woman, as a mother and as a citizen of the world. Now, no matter what my life span is, my existence in this world will have made a difference and my daughter will have a legacy that will never die.

Maimah Karmo lives in Aldie, Virginia. Maimah's motto is "use a challenge as a gift". She is the founder of the Tigerlily Foundation, which educates, advocates for, empowers and provides hands-on support to young women – before, during and after breast cancer. She can be reached at Maimah@tigerlilyfoundation.org.

Hear Rita Roar

Oh, my God, I can roar! I am roaring! At the tender age of 69, I'm finding my voice. And I like my voice. It's kind and caring and happy. It's very much alive and engaged in life. That is, *I* am very much alive and engaged in life!

For most people what I'm about to say is hard to understand, but all my life I lived with the subconscious belief that I had no right ... no right to my own choices and judgment, to my intelligence and capabilities, to my spirituality and soaring spirit, to honor and care for myself, to have ambitions and dreams for my future, to be authentically who I am without harsh judgment, to accept my imperfections and still have confidence in myself, to have needs, wants and desires, to trust my inner wisdom and sacredness. What has finally dawned on me is "Says who?" Who says I have no right?

Well, it started with a mother who was a profoundly disturbed and destructive woman. She started that ball rolling in each of her six children, very deliberately and effectively. But I am the one who perpetuated that insanity. Yes, me. In my work, my family, my friendships, my relationship with myself! Because I believed it! There was no way for me to be an equal member of the human race. To function as an ordinary, extraordinary person like everyone else. That could not happen because "I had no right."

What sustained me was the love and generosity I always felt for others, especially my family. It just poured out of me and filled me to overflowing — in that order. It was the juice that flowed through my life. It was "the God of my understanding" manifesting through me, and I was a more than a willing host, albeit one who was unaware.

I cooked delicious family meals every day, worked full time, managed every aspect of my home alone, because I could not ask for help. I did not know it was okay to ask for help, so I did it all — in punishing and unhealthy isolation. So it looked to everyone like I handled everything in stride. No one knew there was no "me" in the picture. How could they? *I* didn't know!

As you would expect, when I was about 50 I hit the skids and crashed. I was so burned out that everything, down to the smallest thing, was too much for me. I was holding on by a thread. Deep depression lasted more than a year. I could barely stay awake, couldn't stop crying, and couldn't see any reason to go on living. I wrote a letter to me, trying to convince myself that there was a reason to live. And because I didn't have a right to fall apart, I concealed all of this from everyone. Truly! No one knew, including my husband. Somehow it escaped his notice, which is a credit to both of us. I didn't want him to know how much agony I was in, and he didn't want to know either! We were a perfect pair.

This is how it is for someone who has experienced "acute, chronic, complex trauma" for much of their lives. Sometimes people like me perpetuate the abuse on themselves because that's all they know. If your personhood as an inherently worthwhile being is continuously denied, ridiculed and destroyed it's not easy to learn how to love, honor and care for yourself.

But on a routine visit to my wonderful internist he sensed something was wrong, said I needed to talk to someone, and suggested a therapist he described as 'excellent.' He was right; she is excellent, and very spiritual.

Early on she told me I needed a spiritual element in my life but I had no idea what she was talking about. However, little by little, out of my devastation, a miracle happened. Faith grew. Faith in a benevolent, steadfast, transcendent Divine that does for me what I cannot do for myself. All I have to do is ask. And, pun intended, it's a match made in heaven.

I went from being a lifelong agnostic, at best, to someone with a "knowing" that the true context of life is a spiritual one, not a physical one. I had always believed fiercely in the sacredness of the human spirit, such as our compassion, generosity, responsibility, and desire to be and do good. Then one day I asked myself where all those profoundly transcendent traits came from and, bingo, the light bulb flashed. There must be a benevolent divine source!

To explore this revelation I started a journal (my first ever), and it quite naturally, without thinking actually, was addressed to Divine Spirit. Since then my relationship with that "Spirit" has been deepening and growing. I now refer to this God of mine as Dearest Divine, because it is so dear and so real to me. My entire day is lived in that relationship, seeking guidance, wisdom and strength, and the rewards are many.

A few years into my spiritual awakening, when I was alone for a few days, I woke up in the middle of the night and "received" a prayer. I got out of bed and wrote it down and each succeeding night, like clockwork, the same thing happened until I had accumulated a number of prayers. It was not dramatic or startling, it simply occurred quietly. Over the years I've written other prayers inspired by my divine Friend, and to this day, all these prayers move me deeply and bless me with peace and serenity.

A couple of years before I turned 65, I began to ask for something meaningful to devote myself to in the remaining years of my life. I had worked for a living my whole life and realized that I wanted my senior years to be a time to do what would "make my heart sing."

Gradually an idea began to develop that has blossomed into a full-fledged endeavor that is the most thrilling and promising thing I've ever done. I call it *Sharing Sorrows ... Healing Hearts*. It's an online support service for people facing a heartache or ordeal that is more than they can deal with.

We all have sorrows at one time or another that are too big, too heavy, for us to carry. They bring us to our knees, and make us wish that someone could understand the magnitude of what we're facing and how much emotional pain we are in. *Sharing Sorrows ... Healing Hearts* fills that need. It provides a venue for people to connect with others who share their particular sorrow and know what they are going through — which releases the enormous power that comes from people helping each other in their times of need. Connecting on that deep, spiritual level changes how we see life, how we see our sorrows, and how we face them. We go through what we must, and come out wiser and more resilient — and related to each other in a way that sustains us and enables us to live our lives fully, regardless of our circumstances.

So here I am, a senior, living the most fulfilling and happiest years of my life, not in silent isolation, but out loud, roaring, surrounded by family, friends and colleagues who love me just the way I am.

I wish that for you, Dear Reader, now and always.

Rita Lombardo, whose abiding principle is being truly true to oneself, is a proud and joy-filled mother and grandmother to her precious family. After months of prayer for a meaningful endeavor in her senior years, she has found her "life's work" and is the founding director of Sharing Sorrows ... Healing Hearts, a web service that gives people around the world the chance to connect with and comfort others who share the same sorrow. Rita can be reached at Rita@SharingSorrows.org.

Chapter 6: Generosity

***"We make a living by what we get, but we make a life by what we give"* — Winston Churchill**

Women are nurturers, givers and caretakers by nature, so it's not surprising that philanthropy — defined as **the** active effort to promote human welfare in the MerriamWebster OnLine dictionary — is instinctive.

Case in point: consider the results of a 1999 survey conducted by the National Foundation for Women Business Owners (NFWBO), in cooperation with The Committee of 200 (C200) and underwritten by Merrill Lynch's Center for Philanthropy and Nonprofit Management. While this survey determined that U.S. business owners (both male and female) are more likely to contribute money to charities than the general U.S. population is, the women entrepreneurs stood out as highly-motivated philanthropists and were more likely than their male counterparts to serve in leadership roles when they volunteered for charitable organizations.

The Roar definition of generosity is **making a difference for others; giving back**. It's certainly true that every one of the 28 Roar authors embodies a pay-it-forward spirit, as all put pen to paper out of a desire to help other women. The six stories that were selected for this chapter are particularly illustrative of the power of seeing beyond the confines of your own experience.

Many of the women in this chapter share experiences of personal traumas that propelled them to create some form of community (support group, blog, foundation) so others wouldn't feel as alone as they did. Some show how the inspiration to give to others created an unexpected turning point in their own lives. All of them beautifully demonstrate the infinite rewards that come from acting with compassion, courage and bigheartedness.

Meet Katherine. Katherine's dreams turned to nightmares when, in the wake of her first child's birth, she cried all the time and began to have disturbing thoughts. "These thoughts terrified me," Katherine says. "I didn't understand where they came from and had no idea what was wrong with me." Find out how this warrior mom turned months of isolation and fear into a movement that has impacted scores of women.

Meet Erica. On September 11, 2001, Erica's husband was visiting New York City, working across the river from the World Trade Center. In the aftermath of the terrorist attack that turned the Twin Towers into ruins, he watched people jump to their deaths. Erica writes, "Upon returning home his dark journey began." Read Erica's story to find out how, six years later, her commitment to taking back the reins of her family's lives turned into a mission to inspire women who feel powerless to change their destiny.

Meet Jaime. In 2004, Jaime got the diagnosis she feared: Dissociative Identity Disorder (DID), formerly called Multiple Personality Disorder. The diagnosis brought with it panic, fear and confusion. Jaime says, "Not wanting to reveal what was wrong with me to my friends or family, I struggled through my therapy alone." Read Jaime's story to find out how she transformed an isolating experience into a national endeavor to change the face of DID.

Meet Cathy. Beginning at age 12, Cathy used deprivation dieting to control her weight. She gained and lost over 1,000 pounds during a 25-year span. "I kept putting weight on over and over again — the opposite of what I wanted!" Cathy writes. Find out how Cathy lost 65 pounds for good and what she has since created out of the realization that others would benefit from hearing her story.

Meet Shannon. Shannon was raped one summer at the age of 16. She never spoke about what happened, even as her life spiraled out of control in the years that followed. "I was lonely and depressed, hating myself and feeling completely lost and aimless," Shannon writes. Learn how an inspired act of generosity became a catalyst for her own liberation.

Meet Anne. Like Shannon, it was Anne's act of generosity that spurred something unexpected — her own self-discovery. Determined to help her Brazilian friend Gigi return to her homeland after 14 years away, Anne put her business and networking skills to work. Anne says, "Suddenly I realized, in using my power to help Gigi, I was also helping myself to make a shift." Read Anne's story to find out what opened up as she quelled her own feeling of homesickness and helped many more than Gigi discover the beauty of their homeland.

Hear Katherine Roar

I was a happily married woman and a successful marketing executive, blissfully expecting my first child. Then, in September 2001, my son was born and what I thought would be a wonderful experience became a terrible nightmare.

I went from being excited and happy to being lost and miserable. I cried all the time and worried I would never be able to be a good mother. I felt defective, and found every minute I spent with my baby felt excruciating because I was sure I was incapable of making him happy. I couldn't sleep, though I was exhausted. I completely lost my appetite. Soon after, I started having disturbing thoughts — what if I drowned him in the bathtub or smothered him with the burp cloth?

These thoughts terrified me. I didn't understand where they came from and had no idea what was wrong with me. I knew I loved my son, so why couldn't I be happy?

Thankfully I didn't wait long to reach out for help. I was fortunate enough to work for a major corporation with excellent insurance and an Employee Assistance Program. I met with a psychiatrist and therapist, and was diagnosed with postpartum OCD (PPOCD), an illness that is part of the spectrum of perinatal mood and anxiety disorders that includes illnesses like postpartum depression and postpartum psychosis.

With medication and therapy, I eventually recovered. Once I was better, I decided I couldn't stand by and let women feel as isolated and scared as I did when going through PPOCD. When I was sick, I was afraid to speak up for fear that I'd lose my life as I knew it. What if they took my baby away? Would I ever get back to myself again? There were very few places to go to find those answers. Our society is very judgmental when it comes to mental illness, and even more judgmental when new mothers aren't experiencing the bliss everyone expects them to.

I started a blog in 2004 called Postpartum Progress (http://postpartumprogress.typepad.com), with the goal to help erase the stigma of maternal mental illness, share information, and provide support to women who need it. Even in the days when I thought no one was reading, I kept going, reminding myself that somebody somewhere would stumble upon my words and find comfort.

In four years, Postpartum Progress has now become the most widely-read blog in the United States on perinatal mood and anxiety disorders. It was named one of the top 10 depression blogs on the web in 2007 by Psych Central, and I was selected by WebMD as one of four "Health Heroes" for 2008. This inspired me to do even more, as there are still so many women and families who don't know where to go, what to do, or even what is wrong with them. They need to be encouraged to get help, so they can recover and avoid the harmful effects of their illnesses on both themselves and their children.

I used to love my job as a marketing director at Coca-Cola. I really thought I was the queen bee! I had no idea I'd be so much happier doing a job I don't even get paid for (though, don't get me wrong, I do hope to be able to make a living someday!). I'm so grateful that such a devastating experience led to work that is so meaningful to me.

I truly believe that the purpose of life is to take the wisdom we gain from tough experiences and use it to help others. I am amazed by all the women I see who have gone through PPD who now dedicate themselves to helping other moms by starting support groups, manning hotlines, going back to school to become therapists and more. They are warrior moms, and I love being a warrior mom with them.

Katherine Stone is the founder and author of Postpartum Progress (http://postpartumprogress.typepad.com), the most widely-read blog on postpartum depression and other mental illnesses related to childbirth. She is a mother of two, a full-time advocate for women who suffer perinatal mood and anxiety disorders, and a member of the board of directors of Postpartum Support International. You can reach her at postpartumprogress@gmail.com.

Hear Erica Roar

On 9-11-08 I was on the runway at Charlotte-Douglas International Airport. It was 9:45 a.m., seven years and one hour after the World Trade Center tragedy which turned the lives upside down for so many people in our country. I remember that day vividly, a normal day getting my daughter ready for school and feeding the kids breakfast. The phone rang and from that moment on our lives were never the same.

I didn't lose someone that day in the tragedy; our loss was different. We became one of the many families that have lived in silent suffering. My husband made it back to us, but slowly over the course of the next six years, we would watch him live but have no life, which in a way I think is almost worse than losing someone, because there is no closure and moving on is something you live with day in and day out.

During those years I became hopeless, bitter, angry and so resentful because we lost my husband that day even though he was still living and breathing.

We lived in Nebraska and my husband's job required him to travel to Jersey City, NJ, every other week. I had actually just returned the day before from a trip back east to see him. We had spent September 8th, 2001 in New York City. We visited the towers that last Saturday they were standing and had been on the top of the building looking out over the amazing city. It's interesting during the course of our day I had wanted to go to a show and my husband wanted to go to the ESPN Sports Bar and I remember saying, "Come on, we need to enjoy this, who knows when we will have a chance to be in the city again together, you never know what tomorrow will bring." Who would have thought the following Tuesday the face of that city would be changed forever.

My husband was working in a building across the river. He felt the first plane hit. He was on the phone and said it felt like their building was hit by something. His windows looked out directly at the Towers. He watched the second plane hit and the first building fall. He watched people jump out of windows and saw people screaming. He had to evacuate his building but had nowhere to go because he checked out of his hotel that morning and was going to catch an afternoon flight home.

We knew more than they did because we had TV. With the roar of fighter jets flying over and the rumors going around, they felt as though the world was coming to an end. At one point he called home and told us all he loved us and that he didn't know what was happening but if he didn't make it home he would see us in heaven.

Upon returning home his dark journey began, dealing with Post Traumatic Stress Disorder, Survivor's Guilt and severe depression. He retreated into his darkness and disengaged from our family. This was the beginning of my family falling apart.

There are many things to tell about these dark years but this is not about that. This is about our survival and coming out of the darkness back into the light. During these years I struggled to keep my faith, stay strong and trust God. I had long periods where my anger and bitterness took over and only added to the darkness we were already in.

Finally in August of 2007 my husband and I had one argument that caused something to just snap inside and wake me up from the nightmare we were living. There was an exact moment I remember that day when I decided to take back the reins of my family's lives and move forward into something more positive.

I had always been a positive person involved in various organizations and activities. I had always been an encourager and had a desire to make a difference in the lives of others. I was ashamed that I had let his darkness take me over. I began seeking out a way to work from home so that I could help with our financial struggles and still be with my kids. This became another journey of ups and downs, amazing self discovery and empowerment. I absorbed myself in learning how to be a coach and everything I possibly could about starting a business and marketing. It felt so good to feel again, to have a passion for something positive.

In the last year I have built a successful consulting and coaching business and am in the process of establishing a non-profit organization called Women Giving Back. I became a co-author of the book "Wake Up Women: Be Happy, Healthy and Wealthy," contributed to the book "Career At Home Mom," by Debbie LaChusa and am in the process of writing my own book, "Live With Passion, Purpose and Positive Pursuit."

It has been an amazing and difficult road to where I am now, but I'm thankful for the opportunity to turn this struggle into a message to encourage others who have similar obstacles they are facing. My deepest passion is to inspire, motivate and encourage women to stop living comfortably numb and thinking they don't have any power to change their destiny. None of us were meant to live in that kind of darkness. We have the power to make a decision to change the course that we are on in this life.

I'm happy to say that my husband is doing much better and on 9-11-08 I had closure to that dark chapter of our life. I was given a clear vision that this was a new beginning for me and my family. As I looked out the window of the plane that day and it took off going faster and faster, I could feel the evil that had overcome my family seven years ago being stripped away and left behind. I saw a physical representation of shifting from the darkness to the light when the plane broke through the grey clouds into the bright white clouds with endless blue sky. The endless sky was a symbol of the endless opportunity ahead to make up for the years lost to darkness, depression and chaos. I thought to myself, "Let's Roll ..." (God Bless You, Todd Beemer), into the future with a new momentum toward peace and prosperity.

Although none of us will forget that life changing moment in 2001, we can let go of the destruction it left behind. It is time to forgive and begin healing from the wounds. It is time to embrace our new destiny that will be filled with peace and prosperity! It is time to live with passion, purpose and positive pursuit!

Erica Rueschhoff is a speaker, author and business consultant. She is also the founder of MomsRealLifeUniversity.com and WAHM-University.com. You can find out more information about her at EricaRueschhoff.com.

Hear Jaime Roar

It was almost four years ago I got the diagnosis I feared: Dissociative Identity Disorder (DID), formerly called Multiple Personality Disorder. I didn't care what name my therapist gave it, to me it screamed, "crazy." I spiraled into a state of panic, fear, and confusion. All I knew about the disorder was what I saw on the television. I had watched "Sybil," seen "Three Faces of Eve." How could this be me? How could this be my life? What will happen to me? What will happen to my job, my friends, my family? I wasn't like the women in the movies. Surely this was a mistake.

Deep inside though, I knew she was right. As hard as it was to accept, this was the only thing that made sense to me. It explained my fragmented memories, the amnesia of my childhood, and the continual feelings of detachment and numbness to my environment. I decided to stay with this therapist and see what she had to offer. What I learned profoundly changed my life.

People with DID have creative minds that developed an amazing way to save them from the inescapable pain and abuse being done during their childhood. It truly is a gift, a sign of resilience rather than craziness. Unfortunately, the general public doesn't see this gift as they should. The media exploits sensational stories like Sybil and Eve. A very popular crime show recently had a main character said to have DID who was suspected to have murdered a baby. Throughout the show she was referred to as "crazy" and "fruit loops." With every word I was reminded of my secret and why I needed to keep it hidden.

Not wanting to reveal what was wrong with me to my friends or family, I struggled through my therapy alone. I counted on myself for the support I needed. The therapy was intense, long, and very hard work. During those very painful weeks of processing the trauma, I could not imagine my life on the other side of this work being good enough to justify all the pain. There were many times I wanted to quit but my determination to claim my life back from my abusers kept me going.

Now my therapy is almost complete and I have never felt happier. My life is better than I could have imagined. Before I started this process, I was living in the front of my brain, terrified to explore what the rest held. I kept busy and distracted hoping to stay one step ahead of memories brought up by unknown triggers. I feared the flashbacks that waited for me in my dreams. Today, I have access to my entire mind. I know my memories, the stories, the hurts, the sadness, the pain. In finding those things, I also found something unexpected: peace. No more running to avoid myself. I can be still and sit comfortably with all of me. I even found happy times buried under all that pain. They were buried so deep, I didn't know they existed.

I wanted to share my joy of what I learned with my closest friends and family. I wanted to have someone to celebrate with, someone to congratulate me on all my hard work. However, there was no one because my biggest fear was being found out so I told nobody.

I was tired of keeping this secret and having no one to share my accomplishment with. It was time for people to see the true picture of DID, to see me. I was ready to roar from the roof tops, "See me. I have DID. I am a teacher, a sister, an aunt, a friend. I am not just a survivor, I am a thriver!"

I decided to test the waters small scale and look for support from other people with DID. I thought they would understand the hard work it took to get to this place of recovery. My search led me to many message boards and chat rooms but I found them difficult to connect with. I then decided to look in my area for people with DID. I started small by forming one of the only peer-led DID support groups in the country. The group grew quickly.

I watched as the members started out initially hiding themselves, and using false names at the meetings. They wanted to meet in a private location so no one would see them. As they began to understand and embrace the gift of their DID, they changed. Their real names are now being used, phone numbers have been exchanged, and we go out in public all the time. They are no longer hiding alone; they are free.

I then reached out to a larger audience. I wrote an article in a survivor newsletter about the positive side of DID. The article generated many emotional responses from professional men and women with DID, all of whom are living their lives with the same fear of being found out. This frustrated me because we should not have to hide. DID is not something to be ashamed of. We are not any more responsible for having the disorder than we are for the abuse that caused it.

Hearing their stories inspired me to do even more by forming my own organization, An Infinite Mind. An Infinite Mind is dedicated to working with professionals and the public to dispel the myths and stigmas attached to the disorder through education and advocacy. In the few months we have been operating, I am already starting to see the impact. We have been the focus of several radio programs; we have spoken at local and national conferences, as well as various community events, and write many articles for professional publications. Some of the people who responded to the original article e-mailed me again to let me know they have since started talking about their DID too. One by one, we are changing the face of DID.

Since my website launched, all my friends, family and co-workers now know my secret and I couldn't be happier. My friend was interviewed recently and she was asked about her reaction to my diagnosis. She simply replied, "I didn't care. It didn't change anything. She is still Jaime and I love her. "

What more could anybody else want than to be accepted and loved for who they are?

Jaime lives in Orlando where she teaches pre-K special education and works as an early interventionist. She is founder of An Infinite Mind, a non-profit dedicated to education and advocacy for people with trauma-based dissociative disorders. Her passion comes from the hope that people with DID can find the resources they need and will no longer worry about stigmatic fears.

Hear Cathy Roar

I was a fat kid. Beginning at age 12, I used deprivation dieting to control my weight. I gained and lost over 1000 pounds during a 25-year span, trying nearly every program out there. I was optimistic that all the popular programs and books knew the secret to losing weight and keeping it off better than I did.

I invested lots of time and money trying to control my body. I kept putting weight on over and over again — the opposite of what I wanted! I was also developing many health problems while feeling hungry nearly all the time. I was worn out.

In 1990, I stopped the madness: I stopped dieting! I figured out that dieting is the problem, not the solution. I taught myself how to eat, tuning into myself. I developed techniques that helped me lose 65 pounds and I never regained it.

That was 18 years ago. Of all the things I have accomplished in my life, I am most proud that I stopped dieting.

Two years ago I realized people would benefit from hearing my story — those getting heavier and heavier while going on more diets all the time. I developed my health counseling practice, All Done Weighting, and I finally declared to the world that I am the "Anti-Diet Expert!" I obtained certifications as a Holistic Health Counselor and Drugless Practitioner and now I help clients lose weight once and for all without dieting or deprivation.

My passion for natural health helps people regain physical and mental health, improving their lives in many ways.

Cathy Barber, Holistic Health Coach, works by phone and e-mail. A graduate of Brown University, she received certification from the Institute for Integrative Nutrition in NYC. She is known as "The Longest Loser" because she stopped yo-yo dieting 19 years ago and lost 65 pounds "forever" without deprivation. She educates and inspires her clients with her innovative concepts daily.

Hear Shannon Roar

I was 16 years old. I wasn't a virgin, but I was hardly a "bad girl." I was at the head of my class at a small private school. I was the co-captain of the cheerleading squad, and I was dating a three-sport athlete from the public high school. I dreamed of going to an Ivy League college and becoming a veterinarian. I assumed that I would marry my high school boyfriend. It was the end of the summer, and my family had rented a cottage on the lake, as we had for the past several years. My sister and I spent afternoons swimming, lying out on the dock, sunning ourselves and watching boys.

Maybe it was because the guys had a boat. Maybe it was because they were older. Maybe it was just because they paid attention to us. Whatever the reason, my sister, our two girlfriends and I agreed to go for a ride with three young men that we had never met before. It sounds ominous and scary now, but it wouldn't have been an unusual occurrence among the summer lake community. And, until about an hour and a half later, I had never even considered that I could be a victim of sexual violence.

I don't remember anyone ever talking to me or my friends about rape. All I knew about it came from after school specials and the nightly news. Rapists were the men who jumped out from behind bushes and the shadows of parking garages to forcibly assault women. They were the child molesters who trolled neighborhood streets in creepy vans pretending to look for lost puppies and offering candy for directions. Guys like Tommy weren't rapists. He was cute and funny. I was attracted to him, and I was definitely flirting with him. But, when he carried me into the deeper water off the shore of the island, he became one of those men. And as the shore grew smaller and the water got deeper, I somehow became one of those helpless women—a victim.

I never spoke about what happened. I did tell my boyfriend, but he called me a slut and blamed me for what had happened. So, I put it away somewhere deep inside of me and tried to pretend that it never happened. Though my senior year was tumultuous, I graduated salutatorian and went away to an Ivy League school in the fall. My relationship with my boyfriend fell apart, but I soon met someone at school and was on my way to fulfilling all of my dreams ... or so I thought.

I didn't know why, but life became increasingly darker, sadder, and much more difficult. I struggled to keep up with my classes. I was afraid of everything and everyone. I began to over eat, to self-injure, and to experience occasional dissociative episodes. I spiraled deeper and deeper into depression, anxiety, and suicidal ideation and eventually left college. I moved back home with no direction. I began drinking and using drugs.

For the next several years, I drifted. I worked as hard as I could at jobs to support myself, but I never had much. I went from relationship to relationship, purposely sabotaging each one. I was lonely and depressed, hating myself and feeling completely lost and aimless. I was all alone. No one could ever understand me. No one else was like me. That was what I believed. No one could have convinced me otherwise.

That is, of course, until I saw a woman at an education fair, sitting behind a table topped by a display board and brochures about rape, self-defense and a hotline. What the hell? Where did all of this stuff come from? I literally had no idea that agencies like hers existed. Like a moth to a flame, I was drawn to her table. I was in complete awe. I had so many questions. She started talking and, as if listening to a spiritual guru, I was enrapt.

I signed up for the agency's newsletter and learned about its self-defense classes. I enrolled in the next one. From there, I decided to become a volunteer and answer its hotline. I was hooked. I couldn't get enough of this new drug, this place, these people. I didn't talk about my experience. I didn't ask for help. But somehow, just being in that environment, I grew stronger and healthier. I felt worthy, useful and appreciated. I felt important.

After I had volunteered for about a year, I was asked to interview for a full-time position. It would involve providing community education on the topic of sexual violence. It could mean that my secret, my past, my rape, would be revealed. I decided to go for it, and I got the job.

I had never done any public speaking before, and I had never really spoken about my own rape. I stumbled a bit in the beginning, but I was encouraged by the knowledge that I was doing something "right" for once. I was teaching boys and girls about sexual assault. I was giving them the information that no one had ever given me. I could see that in each crowd I was too late for at least one girl, but, for her, I vowed to continue to speak.

I began telling my own story. I became more and more confident and felt more powerful than ever. Even though I was still nagged by feelings of self-doubt, I allowed myself to accept the gratitude of others. I felt that I owed it to all victims to embody a survivor's attitude. And I continued to speak.

I have been speaking now for almost 10 years. I have worked as an advocate and educator in four states. I have spoken to boys and girls in elementary schools, middle schools, high schools and colleges. I have conducted training for medical students, police academies, teachers, and hospital staff. I have done TV, radio and newspaper interviews. I've raised money and awareness. I continue to volunteer on a rape crisis hotline, and I work full-time as an advocate in a probation unit. I work with convicted sex offenders, their families and their victims.

I don't tell my own story much anymore, because my story has taken on less and less importance over the years. I used to track time using my rape as a measuring tool. For instance, when I turned 32, I remarked that I had now spent half of my life as a rape survivor. I looked at myself and at my life as having two separate and distinct incarnations — pre-rape and post-rape.

Now, while I know that my rape was a traumatic experience with lasting impact, I know that it didn't destroy that girl that I was back then. I can never be naïve again, but I can embrace all of the good qualities that I had at 16. I can be hopeful, romantic, silly and flirty. I can dream of the future. I can make goals for myself.

I can lie in the sun, listen to the waves lap against the bottom of a rowboat, and smile.

Shannon devotes her professional and personal life to advocating for victims of sexual violence and raising awareness of the issue. She is the member of two national speakers' bureaus and raises money for her chosen charity, Speaking Out About Rape (SOAR), by skydiving annually. Her greatest joy comes from her family of rescued pets. Shannon can be reached at tjwesson@yahoo.com.

Hear Anne Roar

My connection to Brazil is something of a mystery, but is most certainly rooted in the music. The music of bossa nova evokes feelings of *saudade*, longing, like the ubiquitous "Girl from Ipanema," which speaks of a stranger's love for a woman he will never know. The steamy sambas of Carnival, with their pulsing African undercurrents, conjure up images of the carefree and exotic. Perhaps the connection reaches back to childhood days, when my parents played their LPs of Sergio Mendez and Brazil 66 on our family room stereo. Or maybe it was the Brazilian I dated for a spell in my 20s, who introduced me to the Latin music scene in Washington and taught me how to move to the sensual samba and *lambada* beats.

But I am certain that one particular friendship, with a musician named Gigi, an *accordionista* and singer from Brazil who came to Washington over 15 years ago, has been focal to my development. I met her one wintry night at Café Lautrec in Adams Morgan, a Tuesday Brazilian Night, where she hooked me in with her infectious laugh and some strange new country rhythms floating out of her accordion. Gigi was from the Northeast region of Brazil, a place known for its tropical beaches, laidback lifestyle, and its own eclectic *feijão*, bean stew, of Brazilian sounds — the birthplace of Frevo and Maracatú with their African undercurrents, and various forms of country music such as *Forró* (fa-ho), *Baião* (by-ow) and *Xôte* (shot-shee).

Over the years, Gigi and I talked frequently about making a trip to her city, João Pessoa, the capital of the state of Paraíba. She told me stories of the fishing village where she had grown up and showed me mesmerizing photos of turquoise waters and white-sand beaches. But this all seemed so remote. Both work and money pressures kept our talk on more of a fantasy than reality level - until one April morning, during a joint spring-cleaning session in my Mount Pleasant row house. Like most immigrants, Gigi, a single mom, held down a number of jobs – including one as a housekeeper to augment her music gig income. So as we cleaned, we listened to Brazilian music on my CD player, and I probed Gigi about the meaning of the Portuguese lyrics, so visceral yet mysterious to my Anglo ears. This time it was a familiar song, Jobim's *"Chega de Saudade."* Gigi tried to explain a concept that had no direct equivalent in the English language. "This man sings about missing his woman, and he says 'enough of the missing, without her he has no peace or beauty, only sadness, that never leaves him, never leaves.' A song of *saudade*, very common in Brazil — like the blues. I keep this feeling for Brazil inside me always, Ana."

"Homesick," it occurred to me. Gigi hadn't been back to her home country since she'd arrived in America with her one-month old son in tow. Far from the beach now, she was living in a condo in Northern Virginia, like a fish out of water. And suddenly the task before me was clear: to raise the money to get Gigi back home, back to the beach, back to her people. Gigi had lost her sister Belmira to cancer the previous year; and I sensed her *saudade* for Brazil had gotten even worse since Bel was gone. So I put my entrepreneurial drive into high-gear and organized a series of fundraising *festas* featuring Gigi and her ChoraBrazil (Cry Brazil) band. People poured in the doors of Cada Vez Club to learn samba and drink *caipirinhas* and help our cause.

By June, after two successful events, we were on our way to raising enough money to send not only Gigi, but also her son and three band members to the homeland. Cash in hand, we headed to see Sonya at Solar Tours, and purchased five passages to Brazil. The next week, at Gigi's urging, I returned to the agency and booked a ticket for myself. Suddenly it was clear that I was meant to travel to Brazil too, perhaps to quell my own *saudade* for a land I had yet to really know.

Three years and three trips later, I have discovered a second home in Brazil. And I have discovered my eye. Living as an *estrangeira,* a stranger in a town of few tourists or English-speakers, my Olympus camera often kept me company, allowing me to capture in images what I could not express in words. I was particularly struck by, and drawn to, the paradoxes of Brazil — the beauty and happiness amidst the pain and poverty: a group of smiling school kids piled on a donkey cart waiting at a stop light alongside shiny new Fiats; the red clay rooftops of *Caminho Rosa favela* against a backdrop of modern, Miami-style high-rises in Manaíra Beach; a misty vista of Imperial Palm-lined *Avenida Vargas* on a rainy day, looking more like a Paris street than subtropical Brazil. In the body of work that evolved, I found myself documenting a sense of balance and assurance in a world of uncertainty — something that I was also learning.

I had a chance to exhibit my work in my new Brazilian hometown, before my return to America. And at the opening night party, the locals were both surprised and proud to discover the beauty of their homeland on the walls of the gallery. One new friend and reporter for the O Norte newspaper marveled at how my photos were raising the self-esteem of the "*Paraibanos* who do not always have a very high opinion of themselves." After six months trying to connect, with a limited Portuguese vocabulary, to my new amigos, finally I was communicating through the images.

My photos were surprisingly well-received in Washington as well. Since returning to home in the summer of 2006, my shot *Canoa Kids* earned first prize in The Washington Post Travel Photo Contest, first in the International Visions Gallery "America in Focus" contest, and runner-up in National Geographic Adventure's "Wide-Angle Lens Contest" in 2007. Another shot *Janela ao Brejo* was a finalist in the Arlington Ellipse Center photography contest. And my solo show the summer of 2007 at the Brazilian American Cultural Institute in Washington, D.C, *Saudade Brazil* featured over 40 images of my life and travels in the Northeast. My portfolio of *Saudade Brazil* images includes shots from my latest 2008 trip, and can be viewed on my website at www.anneseye.com.

Ironically, while my friend Gigi found her power in leaving Brazil for America, I found mine the other way around: escaping America and seeing life through a different lens.

Anne Pellicciotto is an Organization Transformation consultant who lives and works in Washington, DC, but keeps one foot firmly planted back in Brazil. On the board of Partners for the Americas, Anne chairs the Arts and Social Action Committee which facilitates artist exchanges between the capital cities of Washington and Brasilia. In addition, Anne is busy working on a book entitled Saudade Brazil which documents in photos and narrative her escape to Brazil, complete with a tempestuous love affair, Candomblé spirit-guide rituals and saudade-infused life awakenings.

Chapter 7: Awakening the Roar

I was at my friend Marisa's wedding during the time we were collecting our first 84 Roar stories, surrounded by a core group of women who have been friends for about a decade. We lovingly refer to ourselves as "The Goddesses." As you can imagine from our title, these are some amazing women. As we gathered to chat at the reception, I asked, "Hey, how are those Hear Us Roar! submissions coming?" The response was uniform: "Oh, I don't really have a story to tell."

There it was, right there in my circle of close friends: the knee-jerk tendency to diminish, downplay and under-represent our own abilities and accomplishments. We don't share our stories because we don't think they matter. And the world suffers as a result. "Ladies," I replied, "this is exactly why this project exists — because women with extraordinary stories think they don't have stories to tell! Do you see the irony here?"

It took just a few minutes for each of my Goddess friends to brainstorm which story she would submit. It wasn't hard and didn't take much time to be present to a moment in her life that she realized she was powerful. What it did take was a nudge, a little support, and the listening of others who often see us more clearly than we are able to see ourselves.

After that, the writing part is a piece of cake.

How Roaring Changed One Woman's Life

Alison hemmed and hawed for weeks about whether to submit a Roar story and, if so, which one to write. When she finally put pen to paper, it led to a huge "aha" about her purpose in life.

> *"I never realized what a difference writing my Hear Us Roar! submission would make in my life — and I do mean my life. The process of writing about my 'roaring moment,' having a natural childbirth in the delivery of my daughter into the world, fostered great clarity for me regarding the difference I want to make.*
>
> *"As a new mom of a 14-month-old, I have been searching again for my identity since her birth, trying to understand how to reconcile my passion and commitment to being a mom with my desire to have an impact that reaches beyond my family. As I crafted the words to share my story with Hear Us Roar!, I became clearer about what I want that impact to be.*
>
> *"I have enrolled in a training program to become a childbirth educator and am well on my way toward making a difference for and empowering other women as they embark on the journey toward becoming mothers. The excitement, joy and levity I feel about this new identity — one that will no doubt continue the 'roaring!' — is truly unprecedented."*

Alison proves that sometimes the greatest benefits come from the most unexpected places.

The Time Has Come to Hear You Roar

It's not too late to write your Roar story or to encourage a friend to write hers. There are many more stories to tell and many more lives to touch.

Visit www.hear-us-roar.com or write to the address below to submit your story:

Hear Us Roar!
c/o Andrea Howe
1725 Eye Street Northwest
Suite 300
Washington, DC 20006
USA

Post Script: Andrea's Story (and a Glimpse at the Roars Yet to be Heard)

There are many more Roar stories to tell, including the more than 50 that were left on the proverbial cutting room floor at the time of this writing.

Actually, it wasn't a cutting room, but my living room. I remember sitting on the floor the day I committed to putting a stake in the ground and once-and-for-all choosing 28 stories for this book. I had procrastinated long enough. It was time to make the tough choices.

I was surrounded by paper copies of the stories, and spent the day (and into the next morning) organizing and re-organizing them into piles. In the midst of the inspiration and the agony of it all, the four themes highlighted in this edition (Perseverance, Authenticity, Faith and Generosity) stood firmly. It was also clear that a fifth theme was taking shape: Self-love. In fact, that's where I humbly chose to place my own story.

Look for future editions of Hear Us Roar! brimming with self-love, including the invaluable lessons and tools that our Roar authors applied to discover the contentment that comes with learning to accept and embrace yourself exactly as you are.

In the meantime ...

Hear Andrea Roar

There I was in the middle of Thailand, traveling alone, and dining alone. I was a 38-year-old woman on her first-ever international solo travel adventure. I was six days into it and had just managed to quiet the voices in my head saying, "Are you nuts? Do you really think you're going to like your own company enough to do this solo?"

My travel itinerary was mostly a spontaneous creation, and consisted of anywhere my "guides" told me to go — the people I met along the way who offered suggestions, sometimes solicited and sometimes not. (Note the breakthrough for a recovering control freak to trust her "guides.")

While checking my boarding pass for an island called Ko Samui, the security guard at the Bangkok airport commented that I'd probably like a different island, Ko Tao, even more. So I listened, and after a couple of days on Ko Samui, off I went by ferry to Ko Tao. All by myself.

It wasn't the first night I had dined alone on the trip, obviously, since I'd managed to eat a few meals since leaving the U.S. But it was the first night I had gotten dressed up (well, as dressed up as you get on a small diver's island in the Gulf of Thailand) and taken myself to a really nice restaurant. I had no book to read, no postcards to write. Nothing to hide behind. Zippo to conceal the fact that I was a table for one.

Here's the unexpected thing: I loved it. I loved the indulgence: I was splurging on me and only me. I loved the pace: I wasn't in a hurry to get anywhere, achieve anything, or to distract myself from myself. I loved the experience: observing, participating, being. Simply put, I felt completely at ease with my external surroundings and my inside world. Both were happy places to be! Maybe for the first time ever.

To say I didn't always like myself, let alone love myself, would be the understatement of the century. For years (as in, more than 30) my internal dialog was dominated by feelings of inadequacy, shame and self-hatred. I was convinced on some deep cellular level that I was damaged, worthless, pathetic, and ugly.

Outward appearances (and a good deal of bravado) painted a very different picture: privileged upbringing, loving and supportive family, great grades in school, lots of friends and suitors, a rapid climb up the corporate ladder. But self-doubt was never far from the surface, always deflating any moments of self-assurance like a persistent leak in an old tire. If I was good enough, surely Daddy wouldn't have left his little 3-year-old "dreamboat," would he? If I were treasured by the universe, I wouldn't have been raped as a teenager, right? If I was a more attractive and lovable woman, my ex-husband would have been proud to keep me by his side, dontcha think? For all those years I waged war on myself; an inner battle declared at an early age and fought valiantly for several decades.

So what turned my war story into my roar story? A series of things, over time. A turning point was the realization during an intensive weekend "self help" workshop that I had been making the circumstances of my life — divorce, rape, and all the rest — *mean* something about me. I came to understand that the not-good-enough-not-treasured-not-attractive-not-lovable chatter in my head was just that — nothing more than the nuclear fallout of all the stories I'd made up as a way to explain things that seemed so unbearably beyond my control.

The key, though, was turning insight into action: I chose to end the 18 years of silence about my rape and speak out in a bold and very public way. The result was a program I created called *Living Out Loud*, a collection of improvisational comedy workshops for survivors of sexual violence who are ready to laugh again. *Living Out Loud* was my way of declaring that it was time to stop surviving and start living. It gave me so many gifts, including the liberation that comes from side-splitting laughter ... and from giving voice to a secret. Through *Living Out Loud*, I exchanged shame for sharing, and war for peace.

Next thing I know I'm a woman on an island, 12,000 miles from anything familiar, enjoying the blissful quiet of a chatter-free meal and the pure joy of feeling powerful and powerfully at home anywhere in the world.

Don't misunderstand; the voices in my head return from time to time (okay, that's a lie, they visit often), intruding like nosy neighbors lonely for company. But now I know that what they say doesn't reflect who I authentically am; the internal dialog is simply part of the machinery that makes us all human. When the threat of war returns, I put those voices on loudspeaker (where they seem so much sillier), ask my cadre of life coaches for support, make a deliberate effort to acknowledge my "done goods" and declare peace again.

I see my life before and after Thailand — all circumstances included — as an incredible journey towards the discovery of my power. Here's a short list of what I've learned so far:

- The stuff I think is so ugly about myself is usually what others find the most beautiful. Everyone is liberated when I share the dirt with generosity.
- Whatever I want more of, I give more of. Time, money, love, everything.
- All that negative self-talk is all made up. And if I'm gonna make it up, I might as well make it good.
- It's not about me. No, really. Authentic power comes from making a difference for others.

The great thing is this: I've only just begun. Now that I've soloed, it's time to fly.

Care to join me?

Andrea Howe lives in Washington, DC and loves that she feels at home anywhere in the world. Her favorite quote is "We are all stumbling towards the light with varying degrees of grace at any given moment." As a businesswoman, she is the Founder and President of BossaNova Consulting Group (www.bossanovaconsulting.com). As a woman, she is the driving force behind Living Out Loud (www.lolworkshops.com) and Hear Us Roar! (www.hear-us-roar.com), endeavors that invite women and the people who love them to live life to the fullest. When she's not working or writing she's dancing and creating mosaic art. Andrea can be reached at andrea@hear-us-roar.com.

Book Club Questions for Discussion

Which story moved you the most? Why?

If you were to invite a friend to write her own Roar story, what story would you want her to tell?

If you were to write your own Roar story, what story would you tell?

What internal obstacles would you have to overcome to write your own Roar story?

What are the social implications of women being willing to stand in their power?

Bibliography

ATHENA Leadership Model®. *Athenafoundation.org.* Athena International, n.d. Web. 4 Oct. 2009.

Lowen, Linda. "Qualities of Women Leaders." *About.com.* About, n.d. Web. 4 Oct. 2009.

Rosenthal, Bruce. "Survey Finds Women Business Owners are Philanthropic Leaders." *Allbusiness.com.* Los Angeles Business Journal, 8 Oct. 2001. Web. 4 Oct. 2009.

"Why Women Leaders Can and Should be Authentic." *Rhrinternational.com.* Executive Insights, Volume 23, Number 3. RHR International, n.d. Web. 4 Oct. 2009.

Author Index

Allene Brack 22

Anne Pellicciotto 103

Cathy Barber 98

Chrissy Turner 28

Christine Tully 25

Cindy Colucci 58

Ellen 71

Emily Hinson 78

Erica Rueschhoff 92

Gillette 35

Ginnie 60

Ina 32

Jaime 95

Janis Goad 75

Katherine Stone 90

Kelly O'Brien 66

Kimberly Whitehead 18

Lauren Malmon 51

Lee Ann Price 37

Maimah Karmo 81

Mandy Gordon 47

Maureen O'Brien 15

Natalie Jobity 53

Rita Lombardo 83

Robin Barbier 44

Shannon 99

Sheila 69

Yael 56

Amplify the Roar!

Book Orders

To order more copies of "Hear Us Roar! 28 Stories of Everyday Women Leading Extraordinary Lives," go to www.hear-us-roar.com.

Bulk Discounts

Please send your requests to info@hear-us-roar.com.

Speaking Engagements

Please send your inquiries to andrea@hear-us-roar.com or call 1-800-946-4395.

Tell Your Story

Visit www.hear-us-roar.com to submit your story. If you don't have Internet access, mail your story to:

Hear Us Roar!
c/o Andrea Howe
1725 Eye Street Northwest
Suite 300
Washington, DC 20006 USA

6038463R0

Made in the USA
Charleston, SC
05 September 2010